Mama,

You Still

Matter

Mama, You Still Matter

A MAMA'S GUILT-FREE GUIDE TO PHYSICAL, MENTAL, & SPIRITUAL SELF-CARE

LAURA HEFLIN

gatekeeper press™

Columbus, Ohio

Mama, You Still Matter: A Mama's Guilt Free Guide to Physical, Mental, and Spiritual Self Care

Published by Gatekeeper Press
2167 Stringtown Rd, Suite 109
Columbus, OH 43123-2989
www.GatekeeperPress.com

Library of Congress Control Number: 2021933866

ISBN (paperback): 9781662909870
eISBN: 9781662909887

I dedicate this book to my husband, Chris. I want to thank you from the bottom of my heart for supporting me throughout my journey as a mother and always encouraging me to chase my dreams. Your support and love have meant the world to me, and I am so incredibly blessed to have you. I also want to thank and dedicate this book to both of my rainbow babies, Scarlett and Carter, for making me a mother and filling my heart with more love than I ever thought possible. You both and your daddy are my world and are the greatest gift from God. I thank Him for you, my sweet family, every single day. I also want to dedicate this book to all of the amazing mamas in this world. You are beautiful gems and fierce warriors, and this book is for you. May you be refreshed and revived by the end of it!

Table of Contents

Introduction

Disclaimer: This book is not intended to treat, cure, or diagnose any individual. I am not a doctor. Always first discuss any new supplement or changes you make in your health care with your doctor.

Mama, I am so glad you are here, reading this book! I truly pray that it will bless you in numerous ways and refresh your mind, body, and soul! But before we get started, let me first tell you what this book *is* and what this book is *not.* This book is *not* a how-to-nail-parenting step-by-step, stage-by-stage kind of book. There are lots of those books available, but this one is not it. This book is *not* a recipe guide on how to help you reach official "#momgoals status," whatever that really means anyway.

Also, I'm sorry to disappoint you, but this book is definitely *not* written by someone who has it all figured out (if she exists, please let me know because I would love to meet her!). In fact, you may find as you read on that it's quite the opposite. Throughout this book I will be sharing the good, the bad, and the ugly, with lots of behind-the-scenes, not-so-glamorous stories with you. I will be vulnerable in sharing my weaknesses, my anxiety triggers, and my "oh no, she didn't!" mommy-fail moments with you as well, because we all have them, so why not go ahead and air my dirty laundry first, right? Of course, I will be sharing lots of my health, fitness, and sanity tips along the way, but mostly, *I want you to think of this book as a tired mama's refresher course on how to refresh herself.* God put this book in my heart to write, so here it is, and I can't wait for you to read it!

But before you do, let me just reiterate that I sure as heck do not have this parenting thing figured out, by far. However, I will say that one thing I *have* figured out is that in order to have all the energy, passion, and drive that good parenting requires of us each day, we must give ourselves lots of self-love, time-outs, forgiveness, and grace. I will go ahead and warn you that I will sound like a broken record by the end of this book, but I won't stop reminding you that you cannot give back to others until you have first given back to yourself, plain and simple. This book is my loving reminder to you that you are worth it and that you still matter, most especially now that you are a mother.

It is so incredibly easy to lose a grip on our health and happiness and let them just disintegrate before our very eyes. It is so easy to lose sight of who we are as unique individuals and as women. It is so incredibly easy to lose our spark, and it is so darn easy to *burn out!* I am hoping this book will be a useful tool that you utilize to preserve and better yourself while you take care of your little ones that I know need you and look up to you so much. I hope this book is a breath of fresh air and the encouragement you've been needing to give back to yourself again.

I myself have been on both ends of the spectrum of motherhood, both miserable and exhausted and genuinely happy and healthy. Because I have lived on both sides of the fence for a significant period of time, I can tell you firsthand that it is incredibly easy as mothers to lose our spark and stamina. I can also tell you, though, that it is *not* an inevitable part of motherhood *if* you're careful and intentional about several important aspects of self-care.

Of course, we will all have hard moments and hard days that rear their ugly heads, but if you make self-care a priority and part of your daily routine, then I promise that you will be able to withstand those harder moments and harder days. So, all of that being said, and if I haven't scared you away yet, keep on reading, and allow me to guide you in caring for yourself physically, mentally, and spiritually. I'd say it's past time that Mama got her groove back! What do you say?

The Definition of a "Good Mom"

A "good mom." Who is she, really? Well, allow me to enlighten you. A "good mom" is *that woman* who wakes up hours earlier before her children every morning, thrilled to greet the day. She is that mom who is constantly found in the kitchen, cooking for her family from scratch. She washes and folds clothes like a boss, and she never lets them sit for days in the dryer. She never has to look for her toddler's other shoe that just magically seems to disappear when it's time to leave because outfits are always picked out the night before and ready to go. She irons endlessly, and her husband never has to ask, "Honey, where is my favorite work shirt?" She dusts and she vacuums, and her house and minivan always smell like a fresh cotton breeze.

She schedules playdates and always can be counted on to show up ten minutes early, with plenty of extra snacks and sunscreen to share. She maintains a screen-free policy in her home, and her children are occupied daily with educational crafts and activities instead. She never raises her voice, gets irritated, or wishes she could hide in the bathroom 'til bedtime because her children are her delight. She recycles and she donates. She volunteers at her children's school, at church, and at the homeless shelter, and she gives endlessly of herself and her time. She is known as "the energizer bunny," and she has no need for that second cup of coffee by the time 3 p.m. hits. She is fit and glowing, and baby weight is a thing of the past. Her style is always Pinterest-worthy; her legs are always freshly shaved. Yoga pants and messy bun days don't exist. She is serious #momgoals in every which way, and she has got it going on.

Hold the phone. Excuse me, what? Is *this* really what you think #momgoals looks like? Do you really believe that in order to do this whole "mom thing" right, you have to measure up to all of *this*, meet some quota, and have all of these boxes checked? Well, funny enough, at one point, so did I. Now, please hear me out. There is *nothing* wrong with any of these attributes! In fact, I still strive to do a lot of these things, but I now know that being a good mom really has nothing to do with how much I accomplish in a day's time, what I look like, or how well my kids behave. The truth is, even on my best days, I am still falling short in one way or another. I never accomplish everything on my to-do list, and something always seems to go wrong, but my perspective and relationship with myself have now changed from when I first became a mother.

The truth is, motherhood is a joyous gift that we often end up missing out on because we hold ourselves to ridiculously high and unrealistic standards, and we always end up being our worst critics. We put these standards on ourselves, and we often get so caught up in giving to and caring for others that we forget to *take* time back for ourselves. More often than not, we end up neglecting our health and our dreams in one way or another, and we find ourselves at the bottom of the ladder. Before we know it, we are burnt out and struggling to just make it through the day, and we no longer enjoy life as we once did. Sound familiar?

We, as mothers, often forget to take the time to hit "reset." Yet, we expect ourselves to keep going at breakneck speed. Well, guess what? I am here writing you this book to let you in on a little secret. You are allowed to take time back for yourself, and you are allowed to hit pause and take time caring for you and you alone because...*Mama, you still matter!*

1 Corinthians 6:19-20 says, "Don't you know that your bodies are a temple of the Holy Spirit, who is in you, whom you have received from God. You are not your own. You were bought at a price. Therefore honor God with your bodies." In a nutshell, God *commands* us to take care of ourselves and maintain our health in all areas physically, mentally, and spiritually. Notice that God doesn't just say to care for ourselves *until* we become mothers. It is a command given to us for our entire lifetime, and it is our job to obey it at any and every stage of life.

This unrealistic picture of a mother is one our society has painted as a woman who does it all with a smile on her face. But truthfully, without an abundance of grace, help, and time to breathe, it is one that is downright near impossible. This idea of #momgoals is one that leads to anxiety and depression and that chucks our confidence straight out the window when we scroll through our social media highlight reel. We see adorable moms with their adorable kids who seemingly love to take pictures in matching outfits on a perfect spring day, munching on the cutest assembled finger snacks. Meanwhile, we are just trying to keep our heads above water.

The truth about being on the outside looking in at a mom that seems to have it all made is that you really don't know what that mom went through to get her children to smile. You don't know the morning she really had when she forgot about the gas stove being on and almost burned the house down. You didn't see the argument she got into with her husband. You didn't get to see her face when she discovered yet another gray hair. You didn't get to see behind the scenes *at all*.

To some I may even appear to have it all. I am that bubbly, energetic woman with a hot husband with a great job, two beautiful kids, and a white picket fence. But let me just enlighten you and tell you that nothing that we have today was just handed to us. We were young and broke as a joke when we got married, living in a one-bedroom apartment with not even a dollar extra to spare to our name. Not even two years into our marriage, my husband's lung spontaneously collapsed, and he had to go through extensive surgery and lengthy hospital stays that put him a whole semester behind in school, and that left us with hospital bills we didn't have the extra money to pay. A couple of years later, when we began trying for a baby, we went through not one, not two, but five miscarriages, only for me to be diagnosed later with a gene mutation that placed me on blood thinners daily, which turned my stomach black and blue my entire pregnancy. No cute bare-belly pictures for me! I could go on and on, but you get the picture. It's been no walk in the park, and we all have our struggles.

Now, in a social media–crazed world, it can be hard to not get stuck thinking that others have it easier than you. Let me just spill the beans now and tell you that as a blogger and an Instagram junkie, I can tell you firsthand that you are only seeing the highlight reel. In fact, just a couple of months ago, my son started puking profusely in the middle of a Live Healthy With Laura photo shoot that had taken weeks to prepare for, and my husband had to rush him home as I painted on a smile despite my anxiety, wondering if my son was okay. The pictures turned out beautifully, and I had a smile on my face. You would never have known that, inside, I was just dying to get the photo shoot over with so I could run home to my sick baby.

Behind the scenes isn't always so pretty, and truly, it doesn't have to be. Also, let's not forget that growing up, our mothers didn't have social media or Pinterest in their faces each day to make them feel inadequate and to discourage them. The fact of the matter is that life has and always will be beautiful in many ways but messy at the same time, and I've decided that that's okay with me. I hope by the end of this book you will decide that it is okay with you too.

So, now that we have established the fact that, really, *no one* has it all together, then let's stop being so hard on ourselves and remember that we are all in this as mothers, together. Now, if you are still feeling down on yourself, let me just set the record straight and tell you that there are a lot of things that a "good mother" does *not* have to do or be. She does not have to be the most organized, patient, or efficient person. She doesn't have to look a certain way, have her laundry always caught up, have her house sparkling clean and she is not required to enjoy every second of every day. None of these are bad things but they aren't requirements.

A good mother is simply a mother that loves with all of her heart and does the best she can. A good mother is one who knows that she is allowed to be human and is willing to give herself grace. A good mother knows that she must practice self care because she knows that if she allows herself to burn out and isn't happy ain't nobody gonna be happy! A "good mom" knows that she must pay attention to her physical, mental and spiritual health else she WILL break. So therefore, she cares for herself and she stops putting herself last.

If self care seems shameful to you or does not come easy to you let me remind you once again that it is a command from our creator to do so, and I hope that this book will help you learn to care for yourself once again, without any shame or guilt, because by doing this you will have the energy to be the happy, energetic, and healthy mother you have always wanted to be.

Look, Mama, I'm not going to sugarcoat it. *Putting yourself last in any way physically, mentally, or spiritually does not make you a better mother for your children.* Your babies may be little, and you may be thinking, "My children need and rely on me so much right now, and therefore my needs and desires must come last in this stage of life. It's just how life is." But man, that's the farthest thing from the truth! Yes, they need you, but they don't need a worn-thin, exhausted and depressed version of you. They need the best version of you to care for them. You are human, remember? Your needs are *exactly the same* as they were before you became a mother, so why are we pretending that they aren't?

So, let's work to change our outlook together. Let's start caring for ourselves again mentally, physically, and spiritually, and maybe in a way that we never have before. If you truly aspire to be the best mom you can be, self-care *must* be at the top of your list. Now, I don't claim to be a parenting expert because I am far from it, but I *can* tell you that *ultimately, loving and caring for yourself is truly one of the greatest ways to give back to your children.* So, let's stop putting ourselves on the back burner, shall we? Let's dive into all of the aspects of self-care together, and let me help guide you step by step in refreshing your mind, body, and soul.

PART 1

Self-Care (The Physical)

Tired. I was so tired. All I kept thinking was, "No one prepared me for this." I went through a relatively uneventful pregnancy, only to find myself in labor for what seemed to be years. Okay, realistically I was in labor for about eighteen hours, but just give me a moment to exaggerate and throw myself a pity party, okay? All right, I'm done now.

Anyway, moving on, I should probably note that due to my scoliosis surgery years at the age of twelve, the anesthesiologist came into the room to inform me that I wasn't a candidate for an epidural. Well, actually, it went something like this. "Here are all of the things that could go wrong if we attempt an epidural, Mrs. Heflin," he said. "But go ahead and feel free to sign this dotted line and we can do it," he said. "Ummm, no thank you," I said. And then that was that. I had officially decided to deliver my daughter naturally... Jesus, take the wheel.

After that, all I remember is that I was beyond exhausted and about ready to beg someone to knock me out with a frying pan. I had Celine Dion on repeat, but really, she was no help (sorry, Celine, I still love you), and my husband (who I love to the moon and back) was falling asleep in the corner. No, I am absolutely *not* still resentful, in case you are wondering. How *could* you ever think that? Okay, I'll take a break from sarcasm for a minute and move on with my story.

So anyway, when it was finally time to push, I felt like I had absolutely nothing left to give. Even though I had my sister and my newly awakened husband (speaking of frying pans, I don't recommend them in the delivery room because someone *will* get hit at some point) at my side, I still didn't think I could keep going. In fact, I actually almost laughed when they told me it was time to push. How in the world was I supposed to exert more energy when I had nothing left in me? How was I supposed to sprint to the finish line when I had been running on empty and unable to stop for a breather, much less a snack (who came up with that torturous rule, anyway)? Not to mention the fact that I was in labor and about to push without any pain relief, and I know, "Women have done this for thousands of years." But let me tell you that that doesn't make it any easier or less painful!

Thank God for that magic aerosol spray that numbs you "down there" after you give birth. I think I went through three cans in the first week! Oh, you don't know what I am talking about yet? Well, that's a whole other chapter for another day, but just jot down in your mommy-to-be notes, "Dermoplast spray equals heaven in a can," and you'll thank me later.

Now, despite how shocking, scary, or familiar my labor and delivery story may be for you, I want you to know that looking back, it is a memory that I now truly cherish. It is still fresh in my mind how helpless I felt. It is still fresh in my mind how unqualified I felt to take care of a new baby. But by the grace of God and His almighty power that I for sure needed, I brought my baby girl into this world, and He has been by my side, guiding me as her mother ever since and every step of the way. Nearly seven years have passed since that beautiful yet grueling day, and I now also am blessed to be the mommy to a little blond-haired, blue-eyed three-year-old boy who melts my heart on the daily.

What have I learned in my journey as a mother so far? Well, first of all, I have learned more than ever how blessed I am to be called "Mommy." At one point in my life, after struggling for years to carry a pregnancy to term, I had lost hope, thinking it would never happen. In fact, it wasn't until I fully surrendered to Him and felt a peace about surrendering to His plan and not my own that I discovered I was pregnant with my daughter. So, needless to say, I am beyond grateful, and I truly would go through the pain all over again as long as it gave me my sweet babies.

Throughout my motherhood journey, I have discovered that there is no road map, no parenting book, no step-by-step Pinterest how-to guide to this parenting thing, and that truthfully, it's by God's grace and coffee somedays that I still have my sanity somewhat intact. I have also learned that, though others will judge you, we will often become our own worst critics when we should be our biggest cheerleaders, so we need to tread carefully. I have learned, as well, that I can't run on empty, and taking breaks isn't optional, no matter how much I want to convince myself that it is.

I have learned to lower my standards. I have learned to laugh a lot off. I have also learned that it's okay to let myself cry. I have now come to the conclusion as well that even though I feel like I am winging it at this motherhood thing, God chose *me* to mother these babies. So if He believes I was made for this, then, well, I have to believe it too. I now have also come to the conclusion that despite my sweet babies that I am called to raise, my wants and needs are still valid. *I am a mama who still matters, and so are you!*

Look, it is no secret that motherhood is a freaking marathon. Am I right, or am I right? It's one of the greatest gifts on earth, but it's downright just draining at times. Kids, especially when they are young, require a lot from us, and I don't say this resentfully. They just do. For the first few years they are solely dependent on us to feed, clothe, bathe, and care for them. It seems that just when you think working overtime at the office is wearing you thin, you get pregnant (which many say is as hard as climbing Mount Everest)! Then your baby is born, and you are told to take it home. "Excuse me, what? Is this a joke?"

This still is ironic to me and makes me chuckle. Despite all the previous infant experience I had had

and all of the *What To Expect* books I read while pregnant, I still was like, "Wait, no, really? This little
baby is totally dependent on *me* for survival, and I'm
allowed to leave here with it and take it home?" Yup,
I quickly realized when we got our discharge paper-
work that they were really serious.

Now, of course, I always planned out in my mind
that we were taking our baby girl home, but then it
hit me that I was going home *without* the nurses and
doctors to ask questions to. Aside from my husband
and my new baby, I was going home alone...yikes! As
moms, when we find ourselves suddenly responsible
for a little baby who eats, poops, and cries at all hours
of the day, it is very easy to get overwhelmed. We ourselves are exhausted and trying to recover from birth,
yet our time is no longer just our own.

Before kids, if we're sick or under the weather,
we will without a doubt find ourselves on the couch,
binge-watching our favorite shows and snoozing for
hours until we feel better. Then we give birth, which
for many is quite an extensive ordeal, and *then* we
are in many ways told by society to just "suck it up"
because "it's all about the baby now." Showering and
sleep become things of the past, and cold coffee and
eggs right out of the skillet become our reality.

If you are yet to become a mom, I will tell you now
that the first few months of newborn life are a hard
adjustment for everybody. They just are. Then, after
a few months have passed, you will find that you are
finally able to slowly venture out of your hole and join

the world again, and you will start feeling a tad more human.

Yet, we often at this stage don't know how to navigate life anymore. We feel lost, and all we know is that this little baby comes first and needs us. Without realizing it, we stop prioritizing ourselves. We try and get away with shortcut after shortcut in caring for ourselves, but eventually our health begins to suffer in one way or another. We need to be cared for. We need healthy food, lots of water, and we need sleep just as we did before.

As we take on our new role as mothers, we must remember that though our circumstances may have drastically changed, our physical, mental, and spiritual needs haven't. Sometimes it is just assumed by even those closest to us that we are automatically these resilient, powerful beings known as "mothers" who can handle whatever comes their way. Yet, the reality of the situation is that we are still vulnerable human beings with needs.

My sister (who is an amazing doula and who helped me give birth to both of my children) once told me that it is very common for a mother who just pushed a baby out, surrounded by family, friends, and medical staff all cheering her on, to instantly find herself *alone* once the baby is born and brought across or taken out of the room to be cleaned up. Now that she, the mother, has fulfilled her purpose, the baby is the focus and all that seemingly matters. Yet, in retrospect, the mother, who just gave birth, needs just as much care and attention.

My sister likes to say that "at every birth, a baby is born, but so is a mother."

Now, of course, it makes sense that the long-awaited baby is the star of the show, but what about the one who grew that baby for nearly a year and gave it life? Oh, that's right. I forgot. Women have been doing this for thousands of years, so it can't be *that* hard, right? I beg to differ. What frustrates me the most is how we bombard a pregnant woman with attention and advice, but then, once she has given birth, she is often forgotten about in the fourth trimester (and often the hardest trimester) and left to fend for herself. Despite how amazing meal trains and pop-in visits are for the first month, after that, a mother often finds herself feeling isolated and alone. It's no wonder postpartum depression is at an all-time high if you ask me. A mother needs to be cared for from the moment her baby is born and then for years to come. She cannot be forgotten about at any stage. Okay, okay, now my rant is over, but hopefully you get what I am trying to say.

Being a mother, without a doubt, is the most rewarding job I have ever had, but it also is the hardest. Unfortunately, sometimes we don't have the support from others we need to take care of ourselves, and then, thankfully, sometimes we do. Regardless of who is supporting us and who isn't, though, we must always be our own advocates and fight for what we know that we need to feel whole, happy, and healthy. A mother *is* a beast and a boss, but she needs her cup refilled too. So, let's break down what that really entails, shall we?

Where Are You on Your Priority Ladder?

Let's get really honest for a minute and answer one simple question. Where do YOU truly fall on your list of priorities? We want so badly to feel and look our best and have energy to do it all, but the million-dollar question is...*how much energy are we really putting forth caring for ourselves?* Abraham Lincoln once said that "discipline is choosing between what you want now and what you want the most." For us to get the health results we want, we must be disciplined; we must put in the work; and we must make ourselves a priority.

So, to honestly answer this question, I like to start with an exercise I do with my clients. Step one is to picture or draw a ladder. Then think or write down on the side the top six things that you are most devoted to and that take up most of your time and energy throughout the average week. Now take a second to look at that list. First of all, are you on it? If not, then, well, we have some work to do, but that's okay. If you *did* make it on your list, then evaluate where on your ladder you actually fall.

Let me share with you what my ladder looked like just a few years ago:

1. My daughter
2. Work
3. House chores and laundry
4. God

5. Me
6. My husband

Wait, are you reading this right? Yup, you sure are. God, me, and my husband somehow all wound up at the bottom of my list, and I am sure you can do the math on how that panned out. I, of course, now know that this wasn't okay, but I am just being transparent with you in hopes that you will be honest as well when building your ladder.

For me, it all came down to the fact that my long-awaited baby was now finally in my arms. Once she was born, she instantly became my world, and she took precedence over everything else. Then, secondly, my job was my next priority. It was something familiar and something that made me feel like "me," and therefore it was something I was unwilling to let go of (even though I was pulling my hair out at the time). Third came my house and laundry that I tried my hardest to keep up to the same standard as I did before my baby was born.

Fourth came my relationship with God, and though I had been such a prayer warrior while pregnant, once my daughter was born, I felt as if I took off running. Looking back, it honestly all feels like a blur. Weeks would pass where I couldn't even remember the last time I prayed. My only last-ditch effort to stay connected to God was to read a quick devotional each morning while I was nursing. Though I did pretty well not missing my morning devotional, the problem was

I had stopped praying. Therefore I ended up hurting my connection to God, and I lost out on the peace He brings with Him.

Fifth came myself. Workouts during the baby's nap, an occasional shower, and prepping myself some healthy lactation snacks were about the extent of my self-care at the time. At the bottom of the ladder was my husband. He got whatever crumbs were left, and no, you don't have to tell me how messed up that is. Trust me, I know it wasn't okay. Sadly, though, messed-up priorities happen to a lot of us women once we become mothers, and oftentimes without us even noticing.

So back to when my daughter was little and when I would find myself eating my toddler's leftovers, snapping at my husband, constantly being on the phone, trying to keep up with my work hours, and cringing when nap time was over. I was always in go, go, go mode, and I was a working fiend. When I wasn't working or taking care of my baby, I was cleaning or folding laundry. I wouldn't ask for help because I wanted to prove to myself and to my husband that I could kill this new role as a mother.

I wanted to get back in shape, so the time I *did* take for myself, I was forcing my body to do extensive amounts of cardio, which in the end left me feeling even more keyed up. Go figure. I was a stressed-out, depressed mess, and if I am being honest, along with my clinical PPD and PPA (postpartum depression and postpartum anxiety), I robbed myself of fully enjoying my daughter's first year of life. My husband and I were also in totally different stages and on different pages, and we lost sight of how to communicate. For a while we just seemed to coexist. While he was trying to find his new normal as a father and in his new job setting, he also was struggling to find the energy to build our new home. In the meantime, I found myself at home, feeling totally isolated away from the world, with a new baby that depended on me for everything.

Now, of course, it wasn't all bad. There were moments that were incredibly special and sweet in that first year of our parenting journey together, like the moment she first said "mama" or began to crawl. But overall, I felt as if I was in robot mode, just trying to figure out my new normal and trying to make it through the day. I was stuck in survival mode, and I was doing my very best to fake it until I made it, which never seemed to happen. What was the missing link? Why was I such a mess in a time of my life that was supposed to be so wonderful and fulfilling?

Well, if you ask me today, I will tell you that, looking back, my overwhelm and lack of zest for life was, for the most part, linked back to my *priority ladder.* It was linked back to the fact that my relationship with God and my husband were hanging on by a thread and that they both remained at the bottom of my priority list. Because of this, we all suffered in the end. But with anything in life, we live and learn, and sometimes we have to go through dark times to realize that we have our priorities all in the wrong order.

In my daughter's second year of life, I was still (and unknowingly) struggling with postpartum depression and anxiety, but something that year was different. I had decided to make it a point to start caring for myself again by first asking for help and making more time in the schedule for *me*. I hired a housecleaner. I backed down on my hours at work (I was blessed to be able to work from home), and I found a babysitter we trusted so that my husband and I could start dating again and spend time mending our relationship. I also committed to praying each morning again after I got out of bed, which helped me start each day off on a positive, less anxious note.

All in all, moving God, my husband, and *myself* back up on my priority ladder was one of the most loving things I have ever done for myself and my family. I was overall in a better place and better able to handle life despite my postpartum hormonal ups and downs, and I was happier for those I loved.

So what about you? What are the top six priorities on your list, and where do *you* fall on the ladder? If you find yourself to be at the bottom of the ladder, then let's pinpoint what needs to happen to move you back up to the top. Sound good?

Taking Ownership of Your Health

So, I have some not-so-great news for you. Those in your household may never lead the healthy life that you hope they would or that you hope to live for yourself. Now, in regards to your kids, of course, you have some say. But if your significant other or other adults you live with constantly seem to be self-sabotaging in the way that they feed themselves or in their lack of self-care, then I have to be frank with you and tell you that that is not your problem. I repeat, that is not your problem. You must stop waiting for them to change in order for you to make changes towards a healthier you. *You deserve love and care today and not tomorrow or next month or next year.*

Going on nine years now as a nutritional consultant, I have averaged that 75 percent of my consultations begin with, "He or she is always bringing in junk food into our house." Or "He or she has no discipline to work out." As their consultant, it is up to me to lovingly remind my clients that they are their own person, and they owe it to themselves to make these healthy changes, despite how others in their home choose to live. As mothers, we often put ourselves last, and we struggle to care for ourselves because so many others depend on us. One thing we have gotten wrong, though, is thinking that anyone's health other than our young children (and, of course, those in our lives with disabilities and illnesses under our care) is our responsibility. Because it's not.

I speak about this topic from a very personal level. My husband is the man of my dreams and the love of my life, and he is a total hottie in my book, but he is without a doubt the most unhealthy eater I have ever met. (He gave me permission to tell you this. *wink wink*) I used to stress over his health and his horrible diet, and at one point early on in our marriage, I ate garbage right alongside him. Nowadays, though, it's just our ongoing joke. See, I one day realized that even though I can offer to make him healthy meals, schedule his doctor's appointments, and lay out his supplements, it is ultimately up to *him* to take the initiative to actually do it. The times when he does make small strides toward bettering his health make me so incredibly happy. On the flipside, the many times he chooses not to care for himself do not change how I, as an individual and as an adult, choose to care for *myself*.

Would it be easier to live with a fellow health junkie? I wouldn't know, but I am sure it would be. Yet, I don't let the fact that my husband isn't health conscious with what he eats (he does go to the gym, so I am proud of him for that) change my perspective and lessen the effort that I put toward my own health. If you, right now, are struggling to find the motivation to care for yourself because your partner or roommate doesn't have the same health goals in mind, then I urge you to *stop waiting on another person to be the wind in your sails and start taking charge of your health today!* You deserve to feel your best, and if you are a mother, you absolutely need to feel your best in order to care for your babies. Do it for them, but first and foremost, do it for yourself, because *Mama, you still matter!*

So let's get right to it! Let's break down the many aspects that make up one's physical health. When you take into account the news, social media, magazines, and blogs, "healthy living" can seem overwhelming, and at times you may feel as if you are on information overload. This is the reason that I developed the Live Healthy With Laura lifestyle, in order to simplify the process and give you lasting results. In this book, though, I am specifically targeting mothers because I believe we have many needs that are often unique to the stage we are in. So, keep on reading to learn more!

Let's Talk Nutrition

You are what you eat. I know it sounds cliché and a bit obnoxious to hear, but it's true. What you feed your body *will* determine how you feel. It *will* affect how your body handles stress, how often you get sick and recover, and yes, it *will* affect how you fit into your mom jeans. Do you find yourself living off of your kid's leftovers? Do you find yourself thinking and planning out your children's snacks, yet you rarely plan what YOU are going to eat ahead of time? Well then, it's time to change that! You have got to stop being an after-thought, my friend!

Nutrition doesn't have to be complicated. It actually can be quite simple, and if you take the tips I am about to share with you into consideration, I think you will find that you, too, can eat well and still juggle mom life if you are intentional about it. It just takes a little strategic planning, and it just takes making yourself more of a priority, because again, let me remind you that, *Mama, you still matter.* See? I warned you I was going to sound like a broken record! Okay, so moving on, here are my top six tips that I believe will leave you feeling happy, healthy, and energized:

Tip #1: Plan ahead...and not just for your kids!

My rule of thumb is if your kids are eating or snacking, then you should be too. If you are thinking of what snacks to pack in the diaper bag for the kids, you should be thinking about your snacks too. Why should you go without? Why should you go around hungry, hangry, and with low blood sugar? If you are a mom, you are putting out a lot of energy, so give your body what it needs in regular increments to keep up with your kids!

So don't leave the house without your own personal snack and water bottle. Don't grocery shop without also thinking ahead of time about what you should be eating as well. Try your best to always have a list and a meal plan for the week, and whatever you do, don't impulse buy junk you will regret later. Don't forget that you, too, need to eat well, and you have to plan ahead for that to happen. Feel free to take all the help you can get by using Instacart, Walmart grocery pickup, etc., to make it easier on you.

I used to drag my kids into the grocery store and spend two hours trying to shop, think straight, and keep them happy. Not anymore though! Once I discovered how magical it was to have my groceries delivered to my front door, I never went back. *I shamelessly take all the shortcuts and the help I can get, and I am a more sane mama because of it!*

Tip #2: Cook in bulk

I get it. Life is crazy, and you are thinking, "I just don't have the time." Guess what? No one feels like they have the time. But you *do* have to eat, and ideally you need to be eating as healthily as possible to keep your energy up. So my advice to you is this: cook once and eat twice.

You can easily have breakfasts and lunches for an entire week ready in the fridge, but this does require devoting at least an hour in the kitchen every single weekend to prep. If you want to follow an easy, delicious meal plan, check out the one in my last book, *Live Healthy With Laura*, where I have it all mapped out for you!

Some of my favorite simple meal and snack ideas that can be easily prepped ahead of time are:

- gluten-free muffins
- granola or energy bars
- overnight oats
- energy balls
- hard-boiled eggs
- Instant Pot brown or wild rice
- Instant Pot beans
- dice up fresh fruit and veggies
- iced tea or infused water sweetened with stevia or monk fruit
- gluten-free, refined-sugar-free cookies or brownies.

You can find recipes for almost all of the above and more on my website www.livehealthywithlaura.com, and I promise you, if you give one or two a try, you will realize how simple and efficient prepping ahead of time on the weekends can be! A little planning and prepping ahead sets you up for a successful, healthy week! Love yourself enough to take that time for *you* on the weekends!

Tip #3: Drink more water

I am sure you think you drink enough water. Most people do until they actually start measuring it out and realize their teeny-tiny sips here and there all day long only equaled about the amount of a sixteen-ounce water bottle. You need *lots* of water to stay healthy, feel your best, and stay fit. When I say "lots" I mean half your body weight in ounces a day(plus more if you're breastfeeding)! Do yourself a favor and make it simple by purchasing a glass or stainless steel (not plastic) liter water bottle and drink at least three a day. You won't believe how much better you look and feel!

Tip #4: Limit the alcohol and caffeine

I want you to know that if you have personal or religious beliefs against alcohol I totally respect that. But in our household we believe that in moderation it is okay for us. After all, Jesus drank wine so we feel that we are okay having a little too but again, we don't have to agree on this. Okay, so that disclaimer aside, haven't we all just had a day when we announce at the end of it "phew! Mama needs a pick me up (or a drink, or dark chocolate or a Netflix binging session)!" If I am being honest after my second child was born and I was left to navigate a very rambunctious toddler and a baby who desperately needed to move up the growth chart all while my husband worked two jobs, I myself drank wine about every night for six months straight. It became an unhealthy coping mechanism and you know what happened? I completely backfired on myself and my health and I ended up moody as ever with a lovely extra layer of fat on my mid section. It wasn't until I pinpointed that it was the wine causing me to feel so off and put on the extra weight that I decided to go completely off of it for a while. I knew the facts but I guess at the time I was so overwhelmed and stressed I just didn't care. It was a coping mechanism that I wasn't proud of but it just took the edge off for a few minutes. It wasn't until one day I started noticing a yucky pattern of bloat, irritability and sore breasts. What does wine have to do with all of this? Well alcohol in general and red wine (thanks the resveratrol) especially, raises estrogen levels within the body. When not properly controlled and balanced, you're left with something called "estrogen dominance," and it isn't pretty. I could go on forever about it, but that is going to have to be another book for another day. In a nutshell, it leaves you a bloated, achy, and cranky mess.

My go-to-now, and what I believe is a good balance, is one to two glasses a week of wine or an alcoholic maximum. I know this may be disappointing to some to read, but trust me on this. The same goes for coffee and caffeine. My rule of thumb is one cup of coffee a day before noon. Caffeine is a stimulant, and therefore it leaves you tired yet wired. The energy you get from caffeine is, in a sense, artificial. It can increase your anxiety and cause you to feel more flustered, which no one needs! Also, though one cup can usually be enjoyed without any issues (for most people), it *can* cause adrenal fatigue, which then can lead to severe hormonal imbalances and weight gain. It can also make heartburn much worse, which, for most pregnant mamas, is already an issue. So I urge you to lower your alcohol and caffeine intake, increase your water consumption, and you will feel like a new woman!

Tip #5: Save room for sweets

Friend, please stop eyeing your kid's popsicle or cookie and drooling over it because you are so sweet deprived and desperately trying to lose weight! Listen, life is short, and you deserve to enjoy life too! If you read my last book or follow me on social media, then you already know that I follow an 80/20 philosophy. The reason this philosophy works is because you allow yourselves to eat what you crave in moderation, thus eliminating your cravings. I think it is important to allow ourselves some wiggle room and not be overly strict with ourselves.

So, though I am not a big advocate for calorie counting, I suggest you do a little food-label reading and give yourself a little daily treat of about two hundred calories or less. For me, it is almost always sea-salt dark chocolate. Just two or three squares and a can of chilled grapefruit sparkling water are my go-to after my kids go to bed. Then, once a week, on date night or girls' night out, I will totally splurge and enjoy an indulgent dinner, a fun beverage, and dessert and not think twice about it. If I don't manage to sneak away that week, we generally will order takeout instead. Other than that, I do eat clean, whole foods, and I avoid gluten and dairy in my "eighty" window. However, I don't obsess over every little bite I eat. I live my life, and I refuse to walk on a tightrope, and so should you, Mama!

Tip #6: Eat often, but eat small

It is no secret that motherhood is a marathon. Starting from pregnancy, through infancy, through those crazy toddler years and on up, it is inevitable that motherhood will take a lot out of you. Therefore, you need constant fuel. Food is fuel, and you need lots of it, but *not* in one sitting and *not* after not eating all day. You need small, frequent meals all day long. Not only does this fire up your metabolism and help you burn fat all day long, but it also keeps your glucose stable and keeps you from crashing and reaching for that third cup of coffee or that handful of chips.

Embracing an 80/20 Mindset

Do you want to know what I find exhausting more than anything? *Trying to be perfect.* In fact, I don't think anything could be more of a recipe for depression than setting unrealistic goals and too-high standards for ourselves in any sense, including our diet, exercise, how we run our homes, our relationships, and so on. Setting our standards too high can leave us feeling like constant failures, especially as mothers. Even if we, for a while, can meet these crazy-ambitious goals, eventually we burn out and lose our confidence in ourselves. We end up asking ourselves, "Why do I even try?"

This is where the 80/20 principle and mindset come in. Now, if you read my last book, you may think I am just getting ready to repeat myself again, but in actuality, I'm not. In this chapter I want to put a different spin on it and explain to you what I think "balance" in life really means and how the 80/20 principle can apply.

Okay, so to give you an analogy, let's take a college exam as an example. You want so badly to get an A, right? Yet, this class is freaking hard! You could sacrifice sleep, food, water, friends, and your sanity to study all day and all night, but you don't want to live in misery. So, what do you do? You aim for a B or B minus instead. Now, maybe this won't get you recognized as "student of the year," but it allows you to maintain balance and enjoyment in your life and still hold onto your sanity at the same time. This doesn't mean that you full-on swing the other way, light a bonfire, and burn your textbooks so you can go out and party all night. But it *does* mean that you allow yourself an allotted amount of time to study and then an allotted amount of time to spend doing other things you need to do, including enjoying your life.

So now, let's take this analogy and apply it to a few other areas. Take food, for example. Eighty percent of the time, clean eating is your goal, but then 20 percent of the time, you relax and eat whatever your heart desires. Think maybe a small treat a day and then a splurge meal per week. You work hard to diligently give your body the nutrients it needs most of the time, but then sometimes you polish off a bowl of cheesy chicken alfredo and a piece of chocolate cake. It's not a big deal, and there is no serious harm done.

Let's move on to parenting. Most of the time, I am sure you probably try and feed your kids a colorful, wholesome diet, ensure that they are getting plenty of fresh air outdoors, away from the TV, and are getting a proper amount of sleep. But then sometimes life gets crazy and you are on a work call and just need the kids to behave, so you toss fruit snacks, an iPad, or whatever you can their way, just to keep them quiet. Or how about those nights when you start a family movie too late, only to realize it is an hour and a half past the kids' bedtime once it's done, and on a school night, for that matter (this happens in our house quite a bit, it seems). You quickly toss them in bed without brushing their teeth and bid them good night. Whoops, parent fail! But really, though, it's not a big deal, and as my husband always jokes, "Their baby teeth are going to fall out anyway." Ha! We brush the kiddos' teeth extra well in the morning, and we try not to fret about it.

What about the state of your home and the status of your laundry? In an ideal world, the toys would always remain picked up and in place and the laundry would always be washed, folded, and put away. But if you are a mom of little ones, let's not even for a second pretend that this is realistic. Maybe if you are snowed in and unable to leave your house for three days in a row, this plays out to be true. But I think most of us can agree that in the typical week, this just ain't happening. In my house, if one room is clean, one room is a disaster. If mine and my husband's clothes are washed and put away, the kids' laundry is backed up. It's just how it is.

Lastly, let's hit on relationships. Maybe you follow a couple on Instagram that you think are serious #couplegoals. They look more in love and happier than ever. Meanwhile, your husband forgot about date night and ended up scheduling a late meeting instead. Or maybe he didn't thank you for the home-cooked dinner you slaved over as the baby was strapped to you. Or maybe you can't remember the last time he told you that you looked pretty. As you begrudgingly pick up his dirty socks and boxers next to the bed, you think, "We are such a mess."

In reality, you just are two imperfect people living together, who probably just need a few hours of kid-free alone time to eat dinner, communicate, and get it on (yup, sex in marriage is a game-changer, but more on that later). No relationship is perfect, so ignore social media, keep God close, and give each other grace for some less-than-amazing days where you for sure will get on each other's nerves (which is totally normal, by the way, even in the best of marriages).

So, the whole message behind the 80/20 principle is simply that balance and grace are KEY to enjoying life. They are also key to letting go of a perfectionist mentality and living your best life. When you take this principle with you and apply it to how you live and treat your body, you know that you are allowed room to breathe, and therefore, eating healthily and exercising doesn't feel like such a burden. The 80/20 principle promotes a way of living and thinking that is simple to maintain. For me, it has helped when I simply acknowledge that I am doing the best I can, and I make that B minus my goal instead of shooting for that A plus. This principle keeps me enjoying my life and motivated to keep going! Now, are you willing to give yourself some grace, Mama, and are you willing to give this 80/20 mindset a try?

A Side Note for Pregnant and Nursing Mothers

Okay, so now that I have hopefully helped relax your viewpoint on healthy living and maybe even motivated you to kick up your diet and exercise a notch (because you know now you can still allow yourself to eat that piece of cake you've been dreaming about), I need to speak solely to my pregnant and new-mommy readers. *Now is not the time to stress about your weight and that stupid number on the scale.* We put so much pressure on ourselves as women and as new mothers to "snap back," when excuse me! Hello! Our body just went through almost a year of growing a baby!

Whether you are nursing or pregnant, you are growing and nurturing a little person, and your body is working so incredibly hard to accomplish this. The last thing it needs is to be overexercised, deprived, or underfed. If you are craving something, then eat it (in moderation, of course). In my research and personal experience, I have found that if you are craving something strongly, there is most likely a good reason.

When I was pregnant with my daughter, I craved chicken and vegetable stir fry with a hefty serving of fried rice from our local Chinese restaurant, followed by chocolate ice cream at least once a week. When I was pregnant with my son, I craved "man food" and treated myself to a big juicy burger with sweet potato fries dipped in mayo almost every week as well. I ate well the majority of the time, but if my body was craving something, I would let it have it within reason. There was something within those foods that my body just needed to have. So, I listened, and I hope you will too.

By all means, do your very best to care for yourself because you are, after all, growing another little human. However, at the same time, I urge you to not be too uptight about it. Allow yourself to relax a little and enjoy this beautiful stage and miracle happening in your life.

Energizing, Milk-Making, and Fat-Blasting Foods

After two full-term, healthy pregnancies and a total of nearly five years combined of breastfeeding both of my babies, I do have some tricks, or shall I say some foods, up my sleeve that I swear by. These foods are my go-tos for energy, healthy skin (that is able to be easily stretched during pregnancy), and an abundant milk supply that kept my babies fed and kept me burning fat naturally. These amazing, nutrition-packed foods are:

- **Avocados**
  They are loaded with healthy monounsaturated fats that help your body build the hormones it needs to function properly and make milk. They also are loaded with fiber that helps boost digestion, fat-burning, and stabilizes blood sugar. Stable blood sugar is KEY to a healthy metabolism and efficient fat-burning.

- **Eggs *With* the Yolk**
  Two whole eggs a day are an amazing way to ensure your body is getting enough of the B vitamins it needs. B vitamins balance your hormones and help your body metabolize foods more efficiently. They are also loaded with filling protein. Each egg contains about seven grams of protein that helps your body build

muscle and maintain a proper glucose balance. Both of which are vital for fat-burning!

- **Natural Peanut Butter**
A scoop of peanut butter goes a long way! Plant-based protein, for one, is easily recognized by the body. Peanut butter is also loaded with healthy, fat-burning, hormone-balancing, and glucose-stabilizing monounsaturated fats, which also lowers our unhealthy, artery-clogging LDL cholesterol and boosts our healthy, protective HDL cholesterol. When I was in a pinch, chasing my toddler and trying to keep my baby content, I would just eat a scoop of natural peanut butter, and it would keep me going 'til I had a chance to actually sit down and eat a meal.

    Whatever you do, I highly recommend that you never go more than three hours without eating. It will throw a wrench in your metabolism, and it will cause your energy and glucose to tank. So, when extra time is not on your side, and you feel as if you are running around like a chicken with its head cut off, have a scoop of peanut butter. It takes two seconds, and it'll keep you going!

- **Oatmeal**
Oats are an amazing source of slow-burning, vitamin- and mineral-packed carbohydrates that keep your energy pumping and that also

encourage your body to produce milk. While nursing, I made sure to enjoy a bowl of oatmeal a day or a homemade granola bar to keep my supply up. They also are a great source of fiber to help prevent constipation, which is common while pregnant and in the postpartum stage.

- **Grass-Fed Butter**
Grass-fed butter is loaded with healthy fats and omegas that help ensure proper hormone production and a happy, healthy brain. Also, grass-fed butter is linked to weight loss and increased fat-burning due to the short-chain fatty acid it contains called "butyric acid." Butyric acid is a strong anti-inflammatory that helps boost thyroid function by helping transport the thyroid hormone TSH to the receptors within the body.

    As you know, our thyroid is directly related to how our metabolism functions. A properly functioning thyroid ensures a healthy-functioning metabolism. A healthy metabolism keeps your body in fat-burning mode, which then naturally makes losing that baby weight less of a hassle! I eat a tablespoon daily, either on a gluten-free waffle, in oatmeal, or melted in my coffee every single day!

- **Watermelon**
I eat this "summer fruit" all year long. Why? Well, for starters, it's extremely hydrating,

and it's super delicious! But aside from that, it is incredibly rich in fiber, which helps keep me "going" and keeps my stomach flat. It also puts me in a great mood! Now, why would this be? Well, remember, our stomach is known as our second brain due to most of our happy hormone, serotonin, being manufactured in our gut. When our digestion is off, so is our mood.

Here's a little TMI for you. Constipation was one of my most hated pregnancy and postpartum symptoms. Sometimes I wouldn't be able to go for days! When hormones are at their highest, our digestion often slows to a snail's pace. A serving of watermelon each morning with my breakfast kept me more regular. On top of that, watermelon is loaded with the antioxidant lycopene that keeps my skin glowing and leaves me looking refreshed and like less of a tired mama!

Now, as many of you know, I often preach that there is a healthy version of everything. *I believe that you absolutely can and should totally make healthy swaps while still eating what you love.* It can be as simple as swapping out white pasta for gluten-free pasta or Ben and Jerry's ice cream for Halo-Top ice cream. But please, please, don't restrict calories, cut carbohydrates, and just try and live off of coffee. That is a recipe for disaster. When we feed our body well, it has the energy to give back to us. When we let our body know that it is okay and cared for, our cortisol (aka our "stress hormone") stays at a healthy level. Guess what? This is the KEY to natural, happy, and lasting weight loss (postpartum, that is)!

So, eat well, eat often, drink lots of water, enjoy that one cup of coffee each day, munch on some dark chocolate or a little sweet of your choosing, and call it a flippin' day! Don't overthink it! *Your body will transform back to a healthy postpartum shape and weight in its own time. Don't deprive it or push it to the point of exhaustion just to hit a goal. It just worked so hard for you, so be gentle and patient with it.* What matters most right now is feeling your best so you can care for that sweet baby and enjoy this fleeting stage! One day you will be feeling like your old self again, but I can promise you that you'll be missing this stage. I know I sure do!

My Go-to Remedy for That "Mummy Tummy"

Moving on to a bit of a lighter topic, allow me to address the infamous "mummy tummy" for a second. Pregnancy is such a beautiful gift, but as much as it is a gift, it is also equally a sacrifice. Our bodies inevitably change A LOT over the period of ten months (nope, it's actually not nine months) it takes to grow a little human. Most of us, myself included, are left in the end with saggy skin, stretch marks, massive milk-leaking boobs, hair loss, skin changes, and a very sore crotch (can I get an amen?). Despite all of this, I will say it again. Pregnancy is a gift, and I wouldn't trade it for the world. I would be lying, though, if I told you that I wasn't antsy to feel like my old self again and squeeze into my pre-pregnancy clothes after my baby was born.

I didn't expect to look exactly the same as I did before, but I did want to feel like the old Laura and be comfortable once again in my skin. I just wanted to feel like me. I believe confidence, first and foremost, comes from within, but how we feel about our outside appearance *does* matter too. So all of that being said, I would be kicking myself if I left this tip out of this book because it really is a game-changer!

It all goes back to my pregnancy with my daughter. I was in research mode one day, early in my third trimester, about the recovery process after giving birth. I am sure I typed something into Google or Pinterest along the lines of "things you wish you knew before giving birth." I read several articles, but one thing that routinely came up was this very disheartening news: *after you have the baby, you will still look pregnant.* "Yikes!" I thought. That was not what I wanted to read. Doesn't your stomach just "snap back"? The short answer is yes, it does in time, to an extent, but no, it does not happen automatically. In fact, it can take months!

Needless to say, I started researching how to hurry up the process in hopes of being able to fit into a dress for my sister's wedding that I would be in only one month after giving birth. Yes, you read that right. I would be walking down an aisle with one hundred and fifty people staring at me only one month after giving birth. That sounds fabulous, doesn't it? Needless to say, I was honestly mortified when I did the math and realized this, and I was determined to look and feel my best by the time the wedding came along. So I researched, and then I researched some more, and I came across something the French culture swears by: *stomach binding.*

Stomach binding after giving birth is a well-known practice in France and among celebrities such as Jessica Alba and Brooke Burke. The reason it works is because while pregnant, our body produces a hormone known as relaxin that relaxes our joints and allows them to shift in order to make room for the growing baby. It also allows our cervix to widen in preparation for birth. But after we give birth, it remains in our system for a period of up to five months, allowing us a window of opportunity to reshape our body faster than we ever have before. I found this incredibly interesting, and needless to say, with the wedding coming up, I decided to purchase a stomach binder off of Amazon and give it a try.

After my first shower in the hospital, I bound my stomach, and I kept the binder on for nearly twenty-four hours for a total of three months, and then I wore it only at night for the remaining two months. Let me tell you...it worked! Man, did it work! My stomach was nearly just as flat as it had been before pregnancy, and by the time the five months were up, my hips were two inches narrower than they were *before* I was pregnant!

Say what?! I was in shock and awe at how powerfully just a simple belly binder or corset could change my body! Now, I did nurse around the clock, ate well, and drank lots of water. I went on walks, and I did light weights once I was cleared, so I know that all played a role. However, I am convinced that belly binding was one of the best things I did for myself in my postpartum recovery. Not only did it flatten and shrink my midsection and my hips that had widened during pregnancy and birth, but it also gave me awesome back support. Side note: back pain is extremely common while nursing due to the way we slouch over to nurse for hours a day.

Anyway, I wore it under my clothes, and it was barely noticeable. I tried both a belly binder I had purchased online and the C-section wrap the hospital had given me for back support, and I decided I actually preferred the C-section wrap over the belly binder. It was thinner and less noticeable under my clothes. Now, was it totally comfortable? No, it wasn't, but it was 1000 percent worth it, and I would do it again! I walked down that aisle in my bridesmaid dress, and I felt beautiful and confident! I bound after I had my son as well, and it made a world of difference. I highly recommend that if you are pregnant or still within the five-month postpartum window, you give it a try!

Dress Yourself Like You Respect Yourself

You're a mom now, and in the early stages, you may feel as if you walk around with spit-up covering your three-day-worn T-shirt, and you constantly have poop stuck under your nails. I know I sure did. So why, if we're going to end up covered in bodily fluids by the end of the day, would we even try to get ready, right? In those first few months, you are homebound anyway, so why even change out of your sweatpants? What difference does it make, anyway, if you're just going to end up smelling like sour milk?

Do you want to know why it makes a difference? You get dressed every day because, *Mama, you still matter!* That is the reason why, and that's more than enough of a reason. Now, hear me out. This idea of "getting dressed" doesn't have to look the same for everyone. In fact, quite often, it varies significantly from person to person, and that's okay. You don't have to "look the part" (whatever that really means anyway), but you do need to dress in a way that makes you feel beautiful and human. When you do this, instantly you will feel more uplifted. Trust me!

It all comes back to the well-known fact that if you constantly feel as if you look horrible on the outside, you're going to feel horrible on the inside. It's just how it is. All vanity aside, when you get dressed every day, physiologically, your brain flips a switch, and in many ways, gets the cue that it's time to get going for the day! Our energy seems to increase, and our mood seems to improve as well just by taking a minute to make ourselves feel and look presentable.

Okay, but what about those crazy first few weeks when you are just trying to get by? Listen, it's survival mode, so yoga pants and dry shampoo may be a necessary reality for a while. I know for me they were. But that being said, *if it's been a few weeks that maybe have turned into a few months or even years of you walking around, looking and dressing like you have the flu, then Mama, I have to lovingly tell you that it's time to snap out of it!*

Showering and getting dressed may seem a luxury in the newborn stage, but they're a necessity after that. So let's not get this confused. Personal hygiene is never a luxury. It is a human right! In the same way that your husband takes time to shower and your children are kept clean, so should you take time for your basic hygienic needs too. By all means, rock those lounge clothes and slippers, but take time to at least shower, brush your teeth, and roll on a little deodorant. You don't have to get in a cute outfit with a full face of makeup and curled hair every day (unless you want to), but at least keep yourself clean. Again, I will remind you, this is a necessity and not a luxury.

Try and think back to your personal style, hygiene, and makeup and hair routine *before* you became a mom. Think back to how you liked to present yourself. Was it dressy, preppy, sporty, or feminine? What look made you feel most beautiful and most like you? Think about it for a minute. Okay, got it? Great! Then let's get you back to feeling more like the old you! You may have less time these days, but I challenge you to spend just fifteen minutes a day getting dressed and getting ready for the day. Dress yourself in a way that communicates to the world, "I value myself." Set that alarm, wake up a few minutes earlier, and then go and *dress yourself like you respect yourself!*

Work It, Mama!

Who wants to really tackle a workout when sleep-deprived and feeling totally out of their element? Not this mama! But man, does it make a crazy difference in my overall mood, hormone balance, body confidence, and stress level! The hardest part is always getting started, but five or ten minutes into sweating it out and jamming out to my favorite hip-hop playlist, I get in the groove. Then some exhilarating feeling comes over me where I feel like yelling from the rooftops, "I've got this!" Something about working out makes me feel confident and in charge and like I am in my own little world. I don't love it when I am getting started, but I always thank myself after I finish!

One myth I want to address is that you have to work out every day, for an hour a day, to get results. That couldn't be farther from the truth. I know for myself, especially in the infant state, that even if I wanted to work out that much (which I never would), I didn't have the time, and I still don't. Also, let's not forget that when we put our body under extreme stress and workout too intensely, our stress hormone, cortisol, climbs, and we hold onto fat and retain water. When we work out too hard, we can actually end up sabotaging our fitness goals. Overexercising is a big no-no, but so is not exercising at all.

So what's a mama to do who wants results but doesn't have extra time on her side? The simple answer is not to work out longer, harder, or even every single day but to work out smarter. In fact, just move in any way for a few minutes each day, and your body will thank you. Think power cleaning your house or maybe a walk with your baby in the stroller or a few sumo squats with the baby strapped to you for a little extra resistance. But if you are ready to get back into formal workouts, then I recommend, while the baby naps, aiming for three to four twenty-minute full-body HIIT sessions that target all those problem areas every mama knows I am talking about. Then maybe add in a few yoga moves here and there, and you're all set. By doing this combo, you will feel amazing and see results in no time!

Why is this? Well, for starters, HIIT workouts keep the body guessing by switching up the moves and giving your heart short breaks in between. This has been shown to increase fat-burning for hours, even after the workout is complete! Secondly, though it is intense, it is too short of a workout session to put the body into "fight or flight mode," which causes a spike in our cortisol levels. It's the perfect short and effective workout for the busy mom!

Now, if you are unsure what this full-body HIIT routine would look like and are in need of a little direction, then you are in luck! My dear friend and trainer Marina Bonanno and I have paired up to teach you a quick, highly effective HIIT routine that you can do without equipment and from the comfort of your own living room! Check it out!

The Busy Mama HIIT Workout

By: Marina Bonanno

Disclaimer: If you have recently given birth and are under the care of a physician, please make sure you get medical clearance before beginning this or any new workout routine.

As an E-RYT200, certified barre instructor and wellness enthusiast, my primary goal is and always has been to help my students develop a positive connection with their bodies. I have been leading a variety of yoga and fitness classes for the past five years. My primary audience? You guessed it: mamas!

My students' hang-ups are always the same: "I don't have hours to spend in the gym." "I don't have childcare." "I don't have the budget for workout equipment." I'm here to debunk and defuse every excuse you thought you had. You don't need fancy gear, loads of time, or even a babysitter. To complete the following workouts, I ask for twenty minutes, your body, a fun playlist, and some solid ground. That's it! Let's work together to make you the best you there is.

HIIT ONE:

1. *Jumping Jacks*
2. *Bodyweight Squats*
3. *Superman (1-Sec Holds)*
4. *Hip Thrusters*

Perform each exercise for forty-five seconds; rest for fifteen seconds. Take a one-minute break after completing the full circuit each time. Complete each full circuit four times.

HIIT TWO:

1. *High Knees*
2. *Tricep Dips*
3. *Bicycle Abs*
4. *Alternating Lunges*

Perform each exercise for forty-five seconds; rest for fifteen seconds. Take a one-minute break after completing the full circuit each time. Complete each full circuit four times.

HIIT THREE:

1. *"Jump Rope"*
2. *Modified Push-Ups*
3. *Side Plank (alternate sides each round)*
4. *Donkey Kicks*

Perform each exercise for forty-five seconds; rest for fifteen seconds. Take a one-minute break after completing the full circuit each time. Complete each full circuit four times.

NOTE: If you need further instruction on how to perform each exercise, we recommend that you look them up by their titles on YouTube and follow one of the many videos available on how to perform each individual exercise properly.

Stress, Hormone Balance, and the Struggle to Lose That Stubborn Baby Weight

I really don't think we give stress enough credit. It's almost as though we accept it as a part of our life and then sweep it under the rug and forget about it. But then we end up finding ourselves cranky, anxious, blue, and unable to lose weight, and we wonder why. The truth is, more often than not, stress is the culprit of many of the not-so-fun issues we put up with as women on a daily basis. Let me break it down for you.

Stress of any sort, both physical or emotional/mental, causes our body's adrenal glands (the little thumb-sized glands above our kidneys) to excrete a "fight or flight" hormone called *cortisol,* which by now I have already introduced you to. This hormone is extremely important and necessary as it gives our body the agility and adrenaline it needs to run from someone trying to attack us in a dark alleyway. What's not so great about it, though, is the fact that it is excreted in response to stress, but not always when we really need it. I've never personally had to run from someone in a dark alleyway, and I hope you haven't either.

Anyway, moving on. Cortisol forces extra glucose into our bloodstream in order to give our body an extra burst of energy to run from danger. The issue is, unless we are literally running off that extra pump of glucose, our body ends up storing it as fat. So can your toddler having a meltdown in the middle of a grocery store, the baby being up all night, not allowing you to sleep, or that argument you had with your husband inevitably lead to fat gain or an inability for you to lose weight? Yup, it actually can. Lovely, isn't it?

On top of that, cortisol also eats away at our magnesium and zinc stores. Magnesium and zinc are minerals in our body that help calm our nervous system and stabilize our blood sugar and blood pressure. But most importantly, magnesium is a very vital building block of both cortisol and a happy, fertility-boosting, and fat-burning hormone called progesterone. Magnesium and zinc help make both, but what happens is that the body puts cortisol higher on its priority list because it believes that running for our life is more important than being happy, making a baby, or being thin.

So when cortisol is constantly getting excreted by our adrenals thanks to our hectic and high-stress lifestyle and its demands, it literally eats away at our magnesium and zinc stores, which then eat away at our progesterone stores, which *then* leaves us with low progesterone in relation to estrogen. And before we know it, we are estrogen dominant and dealing with yucky symptoms, such as:

- *a suppressed thyroid, thanks to high copper (due to a zinc deficiency), which then leads to the making of more estrogen within the body, that inhibits the body's ability to properly convert the thyroid hormone T4 to the active form T3*
- *weight gain or an inability to lose weight*
- *water retention*
- *anxiety and paranoia*

- *depression*
- *irritability*
- *insomnia*
- *adrenal fatigue and burnout (when the adrenals no longer can keep up with your body's cortisol demands)*
- *headaches*
- *heavy periods that contain lots of clots (more estrogen means a thicker uterine lining)*
- *severe menstrual cramps*
- *sore breasts*
- *acne*
- *forgetfulness, foggy thinking, or "mommy brain"*
- *cravings for sugar and carbohydrates*
- *severe fatigue.*

...Fun, fun, fun!

A few months into my daughter's life, I had all of these awful symptoms. I was walking around feeling as if my mind was racing, and I hadn't slept. I had the worst, most painful periods, and I couldn't lose a pound to save my LIFE! But do you know what I did? I pushed myself, and I worked out harder. I drank more coffee and wine, and I didn't change anything in my life in order to help me regain my sanity and to help me slow down. I could do it all, remember?

Needless to say, I experienced a massive panic attack one day in a parking lot after eating lunch with a friend. My heart was racing, my blood pressure was scary low (sometimes it can be the opposite), and

I could barely keep my eyes open. I remember actually thinking, "Am I going to die"? I called my husband and my mom. My husband came and picked up our four-month-old daughter and brought her to my sister's house, and my husband then met my mom and me at the ER.

They did all sorts of tests on me, only to discover absolutely nothing wrong and to basically tell me, "Honey, you're stressed, and probably having a panic attack." I thought to myself, "Wait, was I really *that* stressed though? I mean, lots of women are moms and juggle what I am juggling every day. Why am I any different?"

Well, the truth is they weren't different than I was. They either knew how to care for themselves in the midst of the chaos, or it's my guess, they probably ended up in the ER having a panic attack like I did. *They just didn't talk about it.* Ask around for yourself, and you will be stunned by how many new moms suffer from horrific panic attacks. It's really quite common. Yet, instead of talking about these scary panic attacks and burnouts, so many mothers talk, post, and blog about the joys of the infant stage, those sweet baby cuddles, the incredible nursing bond, and the love that is instantly there at first sight. They make it look so darn easy on their social media accounts. So as a new mom, who was I to know how stressful it would be at times? I wasn't prepared.

The truth is, the stress in our life, if not properly managed, can have very real and severe consequences. So in this chapter, I want to pass on a few tried-and-true, stress-relieving, adrenal-nurturing, and hormone-balancing tips and techniques I swear by:

1. Allow yourself ONE cup of caffeinated tea or coffee before 12 p.m. Remember, caffeine is a stimulant, and the last thing you need is for your adrenals to be told they have to work harder!

2. Sleep at least seven hours a night (or total per day, including naps). Look, I'm being practical here. Eight hours of sleep is ideal, but it's not always doable, especially in those early stages of infancy. I know everyone says it, but truly you HAVE to sleep when that baby sleeps in those first few months. More than likely your baby will have its nights and days mixed up, so you may find yourself sleeping more during the day for a while. Sleep allows our body to maintain healthy cortisol and hormone levels. It allows our body to reset! Laundry and dishes can wait. Go take that nap, Mama!

3. Ask your doctor about supplementing with good-quality zinc and magnesium to help nurture your adrenal glands and nervous system. I personally love and recommend the Solgar brand of zinc picolinate, which is very easily absorbed by the body, as well as the Nobi Nutrition magnesium complex capsules. Both are found on Amazon. I recommend taking

both of these at night, after dinner, as they relax you and can make you a bit sleepy!

4. Consult with your doctor (specifically your ob-gyn) and ask if they think a natural progesterone cream would be beneficial for you to try! Emerita progesterone cream (the original formula, NOT the lavender formula), derived from wild yams, was a life-saver for me after I had my babies! It helped rebalance my hormones, and it helped prevent estrogen dominance and all of those yucky side effects that come with it. To this day, I still use it every single morning, and I doubt I will ever stop.

5. Avoid synthetic skin-care products that contain estrogen-mimicking chemical compounds called xenoestrogens. Also avoid applying most essential oils directly onto the skin (especially lavender and tea-tree oils), which are classified as phytoestrogens, which also mimic estrogen in the body. Studies show that citrus essential oils do not hamper hormonal balance or mimic estrogen, so they are an exception to the rule, but more on these seemingly "natural" hormone disruptors in the next chapter.

6. Practice yoga and Pilates. Do light weight exercises. Go for walks, and limit intense exercise, which can raise your cortisol and work against your health and fitness goals. Despite what you may have been made to believe, working out too hard can keep weight on you and wreck

your hormones. Oftentimes doing less and keeping your body in a relaxed state gives you better fitness results! Ironic, isn't it?

7. Load up on these three serotonin-rich foods: dark chocolate (60 percent or greater) walnuts, and bananas! These all will help stabilize your mood and help you avoid or lessen those "baby blues"! In fact, black walnuts specifically have been known as "nature's Xanax," and for a very good reason! They contain a whopping 304 mcg per gram, whereas their relative English walnuts only contain 87 mcg!

With all that being said, the point I am trying to drive home is that balancing your hormones and maintaining healthy stress and cortisol levels is really the KEY to an efficient metabolism and a happy, healthy body and mind! There really is no way around it! So, I highly recommend that you try some (if not all) of these tried-and-true tips under your doctor's supervision and see how your body transforms! You will be amazed at how much these small changes really add up and make a difference in your overall mental and physical health!

The Downside of Phytoestrogens

If you are an essential oil lover, please don't read this chapter and think that I am against essential oils entirely or that I mean any offense. My goal is just to bring awareness to a topic that I believe many have not been educated on. The fact of the matter is, many women are unknowingly sabotaging their hormones without even realizing it, and in the simplest of ways: skin care.

So, for me, it all started for me a few years ago, after I had my son, when I noticed that no matter what time of the month it was, I *constantly* was bloated, irritable, and had consistent breast tenderness. My weight also was at a standstill even though I was eating extremely well and was very active. My thyroid levels came back normal, so I was at a complete loss. I was so incredibly frustrated because, to me, I was doing everything "right." Again, I was eating well, drinking tons of water, and working out. So why then did I feel so imbalanced, stuck, and off-kilter?

After months of research, I finally caught on that my hormones must be imbalanced as I had a lot of the classic symptoms. So, I went to my ob-gyn, who tested my hormones (after some persistence on my part), and I was told that my levels were in the "normal range." Which frustrated me even further. What I didn't know then that I do know now is that being in the "normal range" really doesn't mean very much. It is all about ratios and optimal levels. For instance, let's take our thyroid level, called our "TSH," for example. "Normal range" is anywhere from .5–5.0, but "optimal range" is from 1–2, according to most endocrinologists. So, if you learn anything from this chapter, my message is to be your own advocate, do your own research, and never accept feeling like crap.

Okay, so, moving on. After leaving the doctor's office, I decided that I wasn't satisfied with being told I was "normal" when I felt anything but. So I went online and I researched some more, and then I calculated my hormonal range (www.omnicalculator. com can quickly do this for you). Well, needless to say, my progesterone to estrogen ratio was a fifty, which is actually quite low, meaning I was in fact estrogen dominant as I thought!

"Optimal range" is between one hundred and five hundred, so this meant that I *wasn't crazy after all.* My hormones were a mess, and I had my answer as to why I was bloated, irritable, had breast tenderness, and was stuck at my postpartum weight no matter how hard I worked to shed a few pounds. Yet to me, something still wasn't adding up. My diet and lifestyle were on point, or so I *thought,* until one afternoon when I was having a telehealth consultation with a new holistic practitioner.

I was telling him all of my symptoms, with constant bloating and water retention at the top of my list. He quickly asked, "Well what is in your skincare products?" I quickly and passively answered, "Oh, they are nothing to worry about because they are all organic, vegan, and all-natural." "Yeah," he said, "but what is *in* them?" Honestly, I really didn't know. I just knew they were organic, vegan, and cruelty-free. So, after going to my bathroom to grab my shampoo bottle and deodorant, I began reading him their ingredients.

"Lavender essential oils, rosemary essential oils, and tea-tree essential oils are in almost all of your products, and they are a recipe for disaster," he said.

"Excuse me, what?" I asked. I was in shock and confused. I had spent a rather decent amount of money on these products, yet apparently they were the culprit for my estrogen dominance and all of my frustrating symptoms? Yup, they actually were. The truth is, I was bathing myself in *plant-based estrogens,* known as phytoestrogens. And I had no idea. Plant-based estrogens, are of course, better for you than synthetic, man-made estrogens, yet they still act like estrogen within the body. He told me to get off of all of my products immediately and to only moisturize with organic coconut oil and nothing else. He also gave me a list of other phytoestrogens to avoid, as well as a list of products he had researched and deemed as safe for his patients, which I will be sharing in just a minute.

How ironic is it, though, that for years since I had begun my healthy journey, I had been unknowingly sabotaging my hormones and endocrine system with expensive and seemingly "amazing for you" skin-care products? Now, you may be thinking, "Wait, aren't herbs and essential oils natural and derived from the earth?" Yes, they are, and they are incredibly potent and have the ability to be dangerous if we aren't careful. Don't take my word for it. Do your own research on how the body processes phytoestrogens. It may come as a shock to you that your expensive and all-natural products are actually full of "natural ingredients" that are wrecking your hormones, your mood, suppressing your thyroid, and contributing to weight gain. Lavender, for one, was in everything from my hand soap to lotion to my lip balm, and it was causing my estrogen levels to go through the roof! Postmenopausal women may greatly benefit from phytoestrogens, but not a woman at my age and stage.

A few years ago there was a study published in 2007 by the *New England Journal of Medicine* that reported three young boys with enlarged breast tissues that had been exposed to several products over a period of time that contained both lavender and tea tree oil. After that study was done, the National Institute of Environmental Health Sciences suggested that if pediatricians ever noticed one of their young male patients with excessive breast tissue, they should ask them which products they were using.

Now, this may just be one study, but I can tell you firsthand that within a month of throwing out all of my phytoestrogen-rich body-care products, my bloat, irritability, and breast tenderness went away, and I finally dropped a few of those stubborn pounds. My muscle tone was also way more evident. Holla! I also switched to only putting coconut oil on my skin and to these products recommended to me by my holistic practitioner.

Here are my go-to, hormone-friendly body-care and cosmetic products:

- My *body moisturizer* from my head down to my toes is organic coconut oil, and that's it. Yup, just plain old coconut oil out of the jar that you will also find in my kitchen!
- My *eye makeup remover* is also coconut oil. However, I purchase the liquid, fractionated version versus the kind in the tub. I just add a few drops to a cotton round and rub away! It removes all of my eye makeup in sixty seconds or less. It really is amazing stuff!
- My homemade *facial moisturizer* is simply:
  - 1 cup organic coconut oil
  - 1/2 tbsp turmeric powder
  - 1 tbsp vitamin C powder straight from the capsules (I use the Solgar brand)

*Melt the coconut oil and then blend all of the ingredients together with a power elixir or a whisk. Pour the mixture into Tupperware with a lid. Lastly, set it in the fridge and allow it to harden, and then store it in your bathroom cabinet and use morning and night! This combination not only moisturizes (thanks to the coconut oil), but it also rebuilds your collagen (thanks to the vitamin C), evens your skin tone, and helps reduce puffiness and inflammation (thanks to the turmeric). I have been using this simple yet amazing concoction for years, and I love it! It totally gives you that "glow!"

- My favorite clean and toxin-free *makeup* lines are Tarte Cosmetics and Arbonne. Their quality is amazing, and their shades are beautiful. I feel good about putting them on my skin!
- My *deodorant* is the grapefruit scent by Noniko. It is aluminum- and paraben-free. It is all-natural, but it actually works and is great for sensitive skin as well!
- My favorite paraben-, dye-, and sulfate-free **shampoo and conditioner** is by Hair Food, in the "coconut milk and chai" scent. It smells like heaven and leaves your hair feeling silky soft!
- My favorite *bodywash* is by Puracy, in the "coconut and vanilla" scent. I use this on the kids too!
- My favorite *facial cleanser* is by NOW Solutions. I am obsessed with their Vitamin C and Oryza Sativa Gentle Scrub. It takes all of your makeup off while at the same time cleansing and gently exfoliating your skin! It's perfect for us busy moms!
- My favorite *face mask* is Indian Healing Clay by Aztec Secret. About once a week, I try and mix some with organic apple cider vinegar, and then I leave it on 'til it gets dry and starts cracking. I also put it under my armpits as it encourages

lymphatic drainage. I love it, and it leaves my skin looking beautiful, even, and clear!

- My go-to whitening *toothpaste* is by HELLO. I religiously use their activated charcoal fluoride and SLS-free toothpaste, and I love it! It does a great job at naturally whitening my teeth without all of those harsh chemicals!

- The *laundry detergent* that keeps my family's clothes clean and fresh is also by Puracy, in their "fresh linen" scent, and also the Attitude brand in the scent "citrus zest." Laundry detergent is extremely important because our clothes sit on our skin all day long, and with our skin being our largest organ, if our laundry detergent is loaded with chemicals and harsh fragrances, then our body is absorbing all of those chemicals and fragrances throughout the day. No bueno!

So, now that you know which hormonal-friendly products I use, here is a list of the plant-based phytoestrogens, some of which you will often find in your body-care products, and some that you may be eating:

- Lavender
- Tea tree
- Rosemary
- Ginger
- Red clover
- Chast-tree berry
- Evening primrose

- Black cohosh
- Dong quai
- Ginseng
- Wild yam
- Valerian root
- St. John's wort
- Clary sage
- Garlic
- Cinnamon
- Peppermint.

Now, I am not a doctor, and I don't claim to be a pro in the endocrine system, but due to the advice given to me by my practitioner, my research, and my own personal experience and healing, I am a believer that phytoestrogens are potent. They have the power to kick our hormones way out of whack. I challenge you to take a look at the "natural" ingredients you are putting on your skin and in your body.

You may just find, as I did, that when you back away from these plant-based estrogens, your uncomfortable and frustrating estrogen-dominant symptoms just coincidentally seem to disappear. I can bet you, though, that it is no coincidence at all, but that it's down to good old scientific facts. Plant-based estrogens *can* cause disruptions within the body and trick the body into thinking it has more estrogen than it actually has, no matter how "natural" they may appear. So my advice is this: keep your skin products simple. Stick to good old coconut oil and citrus oils, and then call it a day.

To Sleep or Not to Sleep

Moms are supposed to be tired, right? Isn't that what we've all heard and all been told? They all say while we are pregnant to "sleep while you can before that baby gets here!" So we are forewarned that sleep is about to be a thing of the past, and then we begrudgingly accept that toughing it out is what we are going to have to do. Before we know it, our "baby" is two years old, and we still haven't revamped our sleep-hygiene habits. If this is you, then I'm telling you that NOW is the time to change that. Your sanity depends on it!

The reality is, yes, when that baby comes, you will miss out on sleep. In fact, when my babies were born, I don't think I have ever felt more exhausted in my life. Those three months were, for lack of a better term, *rough*! But that doesn't mean that you are supposed to ever get used to not sleeping or accept it as part of your lifestyle for the long haul.

When you are pregnant, everyone tells you that you better sleep when that baby sleeps. But is that really all that necessary? I mean, we have a lot to do! Can't sleep wait? The answer is a resounding *no*. It absolutely can't. Listen, there is a reason that China uses sleep deprivation as a form of torture. Sleep deprivation is linked to anxiety, depression, irritability, increased inflammation in the body, weight gain, and more.

In fact, I have had clients that seemingly did "everything right" in the nutrition and exercise department but could not lose a single pound for the life of them until sleep was back on the table. Remember, your body must be well-rested in order to efficiently burn fat and keep your stress and thyroid hormones at a healthy level. Every human being needs a certain amount of sleep to function. *You can't drive a car with an empty tank, can you? No, you can't. So let's stop trying.*

Trust me, I know what you are thinking. "But my baby isn't sleeping!" And listen, I get it. You often wonder at 2 a.m., while you are feeding and changing your baby and watching your husband snooze soundly, if a full night's sleep will ever happen for you again. You are exhausted out of your mind, and each night seems to be the same marathon. So what is a mama to do? Is there really any way to be a rested mother who is not rundown while caring for an infant? The answer is YES! But it doesn't come freely. It comes with some strategic planning and some discipline on your part. Here are my tips for healthy sleep hygiene during those first few precious but brutal months. These tips worked wonders for my babies, and I am crossing my fingers and hoping they work for yours too!

Note: even if you are past the infant stage, I recommend that you don't skim past these tips. I'm sure that you know of at least one sleep-deprived mama with a new baby that you could share them with. (IF she's open to advice, of course!)

1. Remember that your baby is born with its nights and days reversed, so it is up to you to reverse that. Now, this process may take

months, but if you stick to a routine, it'll pay off!

2. At night, swaddle your baby nice and snug. Lay it in a designated nighttime bassinet or crib. Turn off all or most of the lights, and keep it as quiet of an environment as possible.

3. Before bed, give your baby a warm bath, even if only for five minutes. Soap is not necessary every time, but warm water reminds babies of the womb and helps soothe them to sleep.

4. Try and keep your baby stimulated after dinnertime, until you are ready for you *both* to go to bed. Undress your baby, sing it songs, give it a rattle or a toy (if it is old enough), and try to keep it awake. That way, when you are ready for bed, say around 10 p.m., the baby will be too.

5. Before you go to bed each night, give your baby a "dream feed," which is basically a full nursing session or bottle before it's time to go to sleep. Think about it. Would you sleep better on an empty stomach or a full stomach? Fill the baby up before bedtime and you will buy yourself more time before the next wake/feed/change session.

6. During the day, swaddle your baby loosely, keep the lights on, and allow your baby to nap in the middle of the living room or anywhere noise may be. Feel free to vacuum while it is sleeping (yes, seriously!), have the TV or music

on, and go about talking at the level you nor-
mally would.

7. Invest in a sleep mask! The first few months,
    you will be up more at night, but a sleep mask
    allows you to take a better-quality nap when
    the baby is napping.

8. Make a one-hour nap nonnegotiable during the
    first three months. If you have older kids, put
    a movie on for them, and don't be shy in ask-
    ing your husband, extended family, friends, or
    neighbors for help during this time.

9. If you are drinking coffee, stick to one cup
    before 12 p.m., regardless of how rocky your
    night was. I know you think that second cup
    of coffee will give you an extra boost, but in
    reality, it will drain your adrenals, jack up your
    hormones, and for sure make it harder for you
    to get that much-needed (and nonnegotiable)
    one-hour nap coming your way.

10. Remember that *this, too, shall pass.* Stick with a
    healthy bedtime routine for both yourself and
    your little one, and I promise, it will pay off!

*Now, these are just the things that I found helped me.
Feel free to take them with a grain of salt or to use them all.
Again, I will remind you, there is no right or wrong, so do
what works best for you! Also, don't forget that there are
lots of sleep experts available, as well as support groups
that can help you as well!*

Even when our children are way past the baby stage, we can find ourselves still skimping on sleep when really, we don't have to. We maybe are just used to getting less sleep, or we are just so busy chasing after our kids all day and running them from activity to activity that, at night, it takes us a few hours to unwind. I get it, and I am guilty of this too. We stay up late and wake up early and do it all over again. Yet we find that our hormones and mood are a wreck, and we can't lose weight. Go figure!

So, what can we do to ensure we are getting that much-needed downtime and a healthy amount of sleep? First of all, I highly recommend that you set a bedtime for your kids that ensures that they are getting a full night's sleep (rested kids equal happier and healthier kids) and that allows you a couple of hours of time off the clock before you go to bed. For us, we have found that putting our kids to bed by 7:30 p.m. each night allows for both to be accomplished.

Also, keep in mind that no one, and I repeat no one, can function well on less than seven to eight hours of sleep a night, so we really have to stop expecting our bodies to.

A couple of years ago, when my mental health was at its worst, I decided to really vamp up my sleep hygiene, and guess what? Within a few days of ensuring I was in bed by 9:30 and asleep by 10 p.m. (and not scrolling through my phone on social media or Pinterest), I felt like a new woman! Mentally, I felt more level, and if you can give me a free pass to talk vanity for a minute, I can also tell you that I looked better than ever! I didn't have bags under my eyes; my stomach seemed flatter; and my skin just had a glow about it. I also could enjoy my day-to-day with the kids way more, and I for sure had more patience.

So, regardless of the stage of motherhood you are in, if your healthy sleep habits are slacking these days, then let me encourage you to practice some self-love and make sleep a higher priority. I can tell you from experience that once you do, you will feel like a new woman and never want to skimp out on sleep again!

Trust the Process

Anything worthwhile in life takes time, hard work, and dedication. Sometimes we can be so hard on ourselves when we are reminded by the scale or our favorite pair of jeans that we have yet to hit our physical fitness goals after we welcome our little one into this world. Or maybe it has been years, and you are still uncomfortable with your body and the changes having children made to your body. But, you know what? It's okay to feel this way.

The real question is (as with any problem in life we may have), what are you doing about it? Are you working towards a solution? Are you caring for yourself in a way that should one day equal the results you desire to help you regain your health and confidence? If not, well then, c'mon, Mama. Let's stop complaining and let's get disciplined enough to care for our body the way it needs us to. We can't just assume that a crappy diet and a sedentary lifestyle are going to get us anywhere now, can we? No, we really can't.

But if you are striving daily to feed your body clean, whole foods, tons of water, and are keeping it moving, then by all means, take a deep breath and remember that feelings of impatience, frustration, and setbacks are all part of the process. If there is anything that I preach to each of my clients, it is this: *real weight loss and physical changes often are a very slow process, but if you treat your body with love and respect along the way, it will thank you with lasting results in the end.*

I think most would agree that one of the hardest things about pregnancy is the fact that we, in a sense, lend our bodies as a baby-making factory for nearly a year. Then we are left with the physical changes to deal with and the new responsibility of caring for a new-born baby on top of it. I would be lying if I didn't tell you that I was anxious about what the aftermath would be while pregnant with my daughter. I would often hear horror stories of women saying, "Pregnancy wrecked my body," and honestly, it freaked me out, to say the least. I didn't want to feel like garbage and hate how I looked after I had my baby. I didn't want their story to become mine, and guess what? It didn't.

I made the choice before ever getting pregnant that I was not going to use pregnancy as an excuse to let go and let live. If anything, I chose to use it as motivation to be healthier and more in tune with my body than ever before. Nowadays I am happy to announce that I truly have no qualms against my postpartum body. Do I have a few stretch marks and a few extra curves to show from it? You betcha I do! But overall, I can say that my diligence in caring for myself while pregnant paid off big-time. In fact, in some ways, I actually prefer my post-baby body, and I feel more confident and feminine today than I did before having kids.

So my message to you is this: eat clean, move often, sleep like a champ, and everything else will pan out in its own time. Embrace your flaws, trust the process, and don't forget in the midst of this journey that, *Mama, you still matter.*

PART 2

Self-Care (The Mental)

Are you feeling keyed up, flustered, and overwhelmed on the daily? There's a reason for that. Did you know that overstimulation has been linked to depression and anxiety? Your brain can only handle so much on sensory overload. So ask yourself, when was the last time you took a step back? When was the last time you had an hour of silence in your life? When was the last time you took time out of your day just for YOU? When was the last time you felt that you could think straight? If you can't remember, then it's time to acknowledge that you aren't living a balanced life, and you are most likely on the verge of a burnout.

You can't pour from an empty cup, so why do you keep trying? You need to take time back for you. You need to take charge of your health mentally, physically, and spiritually in order to be that mother you dream of being for your children. You may now play the role of "mama," but it doesn't change the fact that YOU as a woman and unique individual still matter. Remember, *the fastest way to lose yourself is to stop valuing the amazing woman that you are.* So, don't stop.

Okay, so now that we've addressed the physical, let's talk about the mental. Without our mental health, we aren't able to live our best life, and that's a big problem. In fact, despite our seemingly perfect circumstances, we may actually be living miserably and barely making it through our day if our mental health is in jeopardy. Life may be beautiful, and our children may be in the most precious, sweet stage, but if we aren't mentally healthy, we can't take it all in. We may be potentially missing out on some of the best days of our life, and that's just not acceptable or okay.

When mental health is typically brought up, anxiety and depression are usually the main issues addressed. But it goes much deeper than that, and I really want to take these next few chapters to break it down. Anxiety and depression are the result of an imbalance of some sort. It may be chemical, but for some it's simply the result of an imbalanced, stressed-out life.

Many mothers, especially, are pulled too thin and don't even realize it. They don't even realize how exhausted they are because they are running off adrenaline. They are in "fight or flight mode" daily, yet they view this feeling as normal. Moms are just supposed to be tired, aren't they? I mean, didn't all those well-meaning older ladies warn you while pregnant to "sleep now while you still can" for a reason? Yes, and they had good advice. But being tired is one thing. As we have already discussed, newborn life is no joke. But *still* being tired and just about as worn out five years later? No, that's not normal, and that's not okay. But it happens to the best of us.

If this is you, you probably have too much on your plate, and your mental headspace is crammed to the max. No wonder you're an anxious, depressed mess (like I was)! Cut yourself a break, Mama! Take time away from your kids, your husband, and your dog just for YOU. Get your nails done. Go sit by the river in silence. Go lock yourself in the bathroom, and go take a bubble bath. Go shut yourself in a room and binge-watch your favorite Netflix show. Whatever you do, love yourself enough to take guilt-free time for *you*. You, your husband, and your kids especially will thank you in the end!

Time Management

John C. Maxwell once said, "You'll never change your life until you change something you do daily. The secret of your success is found in your daily routine." And I have to say I agree with him. The truth is that neither your health nor a clear mind will be handed to you. You have to make the time and take the time to maintain it. Motherhood is a whirlwind, but there are ways to navigate through it and still feel your best. So, let's get right to it, and let's talk about the variables!

A few years back, I used to not have a single hour left in my planner that wasn't booked. I used to feel as if a productive life meant a hectic and busy life, and I drove myself into the ground with exhaustion. At the time, though, I didn't realize it. I actually thought it was fulfilling me. I used to feel the need to be with people at all times. I never ever was really alone. For some reason, the thought of it depressed me. God says to "be still," yet looking back, I never made time for the stillness, and I never made time for just *me*. Then, when my babies came, I ironically slowed down and found myself alone more than ever.

It wasn't by choice, but more so by force.

I was in a stage where staying home was a necessity for survival. I was so busy up until the moment I had my daughter, and then I found myself sitting on my couch, nursing a precious little baby while scrolling through Pinterest. It was amazing, but it was also quite lonely. I missed my coworkers. I missed being with other adults, and I felt as if I was losing my old self.

It took some time to adjust to my new role, and ultimately, after a few months, I started to appreciate the stillness that I had been missing in my life. Becoming a mother taught me to slow down, and I am so grateful that it did. Living through the eyes of a child, you start to see the world differently. You start to experience the world and see it as your children see it, and you get to watch their excitement as they discover it. I soon realized that staying busy and going to several playdates a week wasn't as fulfilling as just being home with my little family. I started to become a "homebody," and I loved it. But then my babies got older, work got busier, my oldest went to school, and activities like ballet and Mommy and Me classes started. I soon found myself in a crazy cycle once again. I felt myself losing the stillness in my life once more, and it began to rob me of joy.

Then COVID hit in March 2020. Man, God has a funny way of slowing us down, doesn't he? What better way than a universal pandemic, right? We were going ninety miles an hour, and then, in the blink of an eye, we were all together at home and unable to leave. Homeschooling became my new occupation, and it was a huge shift for sure.

Now, if I am being honest, I have to tell you that I hate change. The first month of anything new is always a struggle for me. Even if life was too hectic for my taste before COVID hit, I craved a routine because it made me feel secure and in control (even though clearly I'm not). Once again I found myself being still. I found myself with time to think. I found myself with time to soul search, and I realized how much I had missed the slowness. I discovered the truth, which I had been contemplating for years, and that is this: *losing yourself doesn't just happen. It happens when we are so caught up in the hustle and bustle that we don't have a moment to evaluate our true happiness and our true self.* The truth is we don't need to have every second of every day planned to be happy. In fact, that is a guaranteed way to lose our true happiness. We need time to just be still.

If you want to get more out of life and soak up the beauty of it, then you have to slow it down. I am constantly reminded of this when I see my children's joy in the most mundane things, in the most un-orchestrated of times. Making forts with the couch pillows, playing school, house, or "cooking-sleep-bed," which is what my three-year-old calls it, are some of the sweetest moments I have witnessed recently. The best part is, they weren't planned. They were free, and they didn't require me to pencil them into our calendar.

Because I made the commitment last year to do less; as a result, we all have been able to enjoy life more as a family. My mental health was totally revamped. God gave me a chance to finish my first book, and we made some very sweet memories as a family. So, if you are feeling frazzled and feel as if your children are growing up too quickly, then I urge you to leave some empty spaces in your calendar to slow down.

You don't have to say yes to every playdate or activity. *You don't have to say yes to anything that doesn't fulfill you and bless your family. You have the ability to not overschedule and the power to say "no."* You have the power to be still. Try it, and you will be amazed by how much more life fulfills you and brings you joy! You will feel more vibrant and healthy and ready to take on the world when you take ownership of the time that God gave *you*.

My Go-to Sanity Saver

Mommy brain is no joke. I know I have experienced it, and I am sure you have too. It generally starts with those days that you wake up to your head spinning, your thoughts overwhelming you, and feeling like one big, jumbled mess. Then you realize that your to-do list is a mile long. That pretty much was my day-to-day reality early on in my motherhood career. I often felt as if I was drowning in a sea of tasks with my name on it, with no life vest in sight. I would wake up most mornings with my first thought being, "Where do I even start?"

There was always a child to feed, a diaper to change, dishes to do, laundry to fold, and a client to call. Some days I would wake up, and I would announce to myself, "I've got this!" But more often than not, I would feel as if I was a flustered, disorganized, big, hot mess. Ultimately, constantly feeling this way zapped my joy. I mean, who wants to feel as if they are always running behind and struggling on the daily?

These days, life is still pretty crazy. But I am happy to report that I now have a method to help me navigate through all of the madness, and it's more simple than you may think! It all came down to me realizing that it was up to ME to organize my day and my schedule in a way that would make sense and in a way that was practical.

These days, I make lists, and lots of them. I put my to-do lists out on paper weekly, and each night I write down what I need to accomplish the next day and at about what time, so that way I don't feel clueless and overwhelmed, trying to figure out how I'm going to get it all done.

I'll be honest: I do have a fancy planner, but I typically just use a piece of paper off of my magnetic notepad on my fridge and scribble it down in about five minutes or less. It's no work of art, but it helps me organize my thoughts nonetheless. It gets the job done, and it keeps me sane!

In the infant stage, my daily to-do list may have looked something like this:

6:00 – wake up, nurse baby, read devotional

6:30 – twenty-minute yoga session (Boho Beautiful on YouTube)

7:00 – breakfast

7:30 – dress Scarlett

8:00 – nurse baby and get dressed

9:00 – do dishes and start a load of laundry

9:30 – nurse baby, snack time, pack lunch

10:00 – park date (12:00, nurse baby)

1:00 – nap time, tackle two loads of laundry, clean up main area

3:00 – nurse baby, snack time

4:00 – Scarlett's ballet class

5:15 – cook dinner

6:00 – eat dinner

7:00 – bathe kids and set out outfits for the next day

7:30 – kids' bedtime

8:00 – *Dancing With The Stars*

10:00 – bedtime (power down electronics).

Nowadays, my to-do list on an average weekday looks something like this:

5:30 – wake up, read devotional

6:00 – make coffee and get dressed

6:30 – wake up the kids

6:45 – dress kids

7:00 – make and eat breakfast

7:30 – leave and drop Scarlett off at school

8:00 – dishes

8:45 – leave for preschool drop-off

9:15 – work out

10:00 – snack, shower, and get dressed

11:00 – tidy house, start laundry

12:00 – pick up Carter from preschool

12:30 – lunch

1:00 – Carter's nap time, virtual nutritional consult

2:00 – fold and put away laundry

3:15 – pick Scarlett up from school

3:30 – snack, playtime

4:45 – Carter's taekwondo class

5:30 – make dinner

6:00 – eat dinner

7:00 – bathe kids

7:30 – bedtime

8:00 – watch show and blog

10:00 – bedtime.

Okay, this may be just a bit more detailed than my everyday to-do list, because some of these tasks are just a given, and it may seem like a mundane task to write down your to-do list each and every night, but I cannot even begin to tell you how much it clears the mind and gives you confidence for the next day ahead! I know it seems tedious to write down something as simple as "get dressed" or "snack time," but it really helps me make the most of my day when I strategically plan out the steps, and I can see it on paper.

I may "know" that all of the above has to happen on any given day, but as a working mom of two kids in two different stages, a husband to love on, a house to keep clean, and endless amounts of laundry to do, if I don't do this, I will without a doubt feel flustered and over-whelmed. This simple method allows me to eliminate all my mental clutter, and it gives me the confidence to keep on swimming. You may not typically be a planner, but I highly suggest that you give this simple method a try. It will help you make the most of your day!

Multitasking: The Perfect Recipe for Frustration

So now that we have established how important lists are for a mama's sanity, I want you to know that I get it. I really do. Aside from your daily routine, you still have a million *other* things to do and not nearly enough time to do them all. These tasks are staring you right in the face, yet you can't seem to get to them. They are an eyesore, yet you can't seem to tackle them! So, why not just try to power through and juggle all of these tasks at once as fast as you can...right? Wrong.

Ironically, multitasking is actually one of the fastest ways to go as slow and as inefficiently as possible, and this is a proven fact. So, if we really want to be efficient, we must focus on one task at a time. No one can do multiple things well at once. Most tasks require our full attention and effort, but as moms, we slip into the trap of multitasking because we *think* we are doing more when in reality, we are accomplishing very little.

Okay, so now, with that said, the kicker is still that there is so much to do! So, what gives? The answer that I have found to be more efficient is really quite simple, and it all comes down to three steps:

1. Block out a two-hour window on a day you are home (preferably when the kids are sleeping or occupied), and then write down and prioritize which tasks need to be done and in which order.

2. Assign each task a realistic and allotted amount of time in ten-, fifteen-, twenty-, thirty, or sixty-minute intervals.
3. Press play on your favorite playlist, set a timer, and get to work on ONE task at a time!

Note: during this time, do NOT make phone calls, text, email, or answer the phone unless it's an emergency, and stay on task until the timer goes off.

You will be amazed how much more you get done and how much more accomplished you feel! Now, what does this have to do with mental health? Well, again, when we constantly feel behind or like sitting ducks, it is a recipe for anxiety, depression, and frustration. Everyone instantly feels happier and more at ease when checking tasks off their to-do list. No one enjoys feeling behind and drowning in half-accomplished tasks. In fact, I know for me personally, almost nothing can grate on my nerves more! So next time you are feeling overwhelmed and blue, then follow these three steps and watch how much you get done and how much better you feel!

Now, keep in mind that every minute counts, and it is our job not to waste them. If I am using the microwave, I try and quickly load a couple of dishes, wipe a counter, or refill our Berkey water filter. If I am on the treadmill and just walking mindlessly, then I usually try and take this time to order groceries, respond to emails, or work on a blog post. If I am sitting on the toilet to take a pee, then I will usually respond to my most recent text messages (excuse the TMI, but just keeping it real). You may be thinking, "Wait, you said no multitasking!" But that is not my suggestion for mindless tasks that don't require us to use our brains but still take up time. It doesn't take much brainpower to microwave leftovers, use our legs, or empty our bladder, so these tasks are exceptions to the rule in my book.

Also, while in the stage of nursing my infants, I would try and use that time to respond to emails or texts as well or to read a book on my phone. However, I really don't suggest doing this each time, as those sweet babies grow up in the blink of an eye, and they won't be able to fit in your arms forever. If I could go back, I would have made it a point to put my phone away more often and just focus on feeding and snuggling my baby. It may feel as if you could be doing more while you are just sitting there, but trust me when I say you will one day wish for those sweet moments back.

All in all, the moral of the story is to focus on the literal task *at hand* and not waste a second. Meaning, whatever task that is requiring your hands should be all that you are focusing on at that present time. It takes time to nail this concept down, but when you do, you will see how much more efficient and less flustered you feel! So, go make that list, set that timer, and get crackin'!

The Comparison Trap

"How does she already have her Christmas cards mailed out? It's not even Thanksgiving yet!"

"Oh my gosh, her car is so clean. Mine looks like we live out of it."

"Her kids just sit there through the whole sermon. Mine can't sit still for five minutes without being bribed."

"How is she so tiny after just having a baby? I have such a long way to go."

"How can they afford to go to Disney World every year? It would take us a lifetime to be able to afford a trip like that for our family."

Okay, stop it right there, friend. Stop and erase each of these self-sabotaging comments from your dialogue, and for heaven's sake, stop comparing your life to someone else's. First of all, let me remind you that the devil does not want you to be happy, and he loves to plant seeds of jealousy in us in order to keep us from enjoying our lives. Secondly, I will remind you again that when you view someone else and their life, you aren't seeing behind the scenes, and you aren't seeing the whole picture.

There have been times in my life where I am sure that, from the outside looking in, I looked like I had it all together, but in reality I was in the worst mental headspace I had ever been in. In fact, just the other day, I had a cute picture pop up as a memory on my phone of us as a family of three at a light show around Christmastime, and I showed my husband Chris and said, "Oh my gosh,

I remember being so depressed and numb at this event, but you would never know it by my smile." Trust me, things are not always what they seem.

So, to drive this point further home, and to hopefully help convince you to stop comparing yourself to others, allow me to take you down memory lane and tell you a quick story.

It was a Saturday morning around five years back when my husband was working, and I decided to take my two-year-old on a little mommy and daughter date. I dressed us both up in coordinating outfits and our matching red Hunter boots and ventured off to the mall. We quickly ran into Starbucks and left, me with my passion tea and Scarlett with her apple juice box. I took a picture of her in her stroller, holding her apple juice and sporting her bouncy pigtails and adorable, shiny red boots. I captioned it something along the lines of "such a fun morning with my sweet baby girl." So cute, right? Well, keep reading.

After Starbucks, I took her to the little kiddie play place in the mall. A few minutes passed of me sitting and watching her play, when I looked over my shoulder to speak to another mom. Before I knew it, my mischievous little toddler came up to take a sip of my tea (that I had hardly had a chance to enjoy yet) and then looked me dead in the eye and dropped it all over the floor, laughed her head off, and then bolted to the back of the nearest department store, wanting me to chase her.

I quickly abandoned my purse, my stroller, and my beverage that was spilled all over the floor and went to grab my toddler. Once I finally caught up with her, I quickly strapped her into the stroller so she couldn't move, quickly cleaned up my spilled tea, and then bolted to the car to go cry.

I was a mess, and at that time, I had been suffering from untreated postpartum depression and anxiety, and it was a struggle for me to even leave the house some days. But that day, I did it. I left the house because I just wanted to have a sweet and fun time with my daughter, maybe take a cute selfie or two, and prove to myself and the world that I could handle my wild child in public on my own and look cute while doing it.

As I quickly walked back to the car, strangers smiled at my seemingly little innocent girl, who was strapped into the stroller, sporting those adorable red Hunter boots and bouncy pigtails. Looking back, I wonder if any moms passed by and saw our matching red boots and thought, "Gosh, she has it all together." In reality, I absolutely didn't, but at that time, I didn't know that that was okay.

If I am being honest, I wanted so badly to look the part of a mom who had it all together. I wanted people to see and like my pictures of my kid and my life on social media, and *I wanted others to make me feel good about myself because inside, I was more insecure than ever.* At that time, I was embarrassed by how my toddler acted that day and the scene I made, having to chase her in front of multiple other parents. I remember wishing I could just hide under a rock. In all reality, though, my two-year-old was just acting like a two-year-old, and I was being way too hard on myself.

Nowadays, I know better, and I know, as our pastor puts it, that Satan does not have the power to destroy us, but he can very easily distract us by causing us to focus on others and envy them. In Proverbs 14:30, it reminds us that "envy rots the bones." So my suggestion is to eliminate the source. If social media or Pinterest are a hindrance to you, then maybe consider getting rid of them for a while or at least take them off of your phone, where they're easier to access. *Do whatever you have to do because being stuck in the comparison trap is a miserable existence and one I have vowed to never be stuck in again.*

Some days, I really do feel that I have it all together when, say, maybe I'm having a good hair day, my car is all vacuumed out, and my kids were angels at the doctor's office. But those days are few and far between. And really, I'm okay with that. I no longer expect myself to measure up to another famous mommy blogger on Pinterest or Instagram, because again, I know that anyone can appear a certain way, and anyone can take a cute picture. Remember my story in the introduction about my son puking during my photo shoot? Yeah, trust me, pictures on a highlight reel are for sure not reality.

But you know what? Some of my most precious and happiest times in my motherhood career have been in the most random, unplanned, and cost-free of times that, to some, may not have been "caption worthy." But nevertheless, to me, they made my heart smile. Most recently the times my kids wreck the living room to build forts with the cushions and play make-believe, or the times we bake together and flour and eggshells go everywhere, have been my favorite. In fact, these days, I make sure to caption those times the most. I love looking back at pictures of times when I was genuinely happy because I have plenty of seemingly "perfect" pictures to look back at where I wasn't.

Postpartum depression robbed me of so much joy, and it forced me to paint on a smile every day for years, yet no one on the outside really knew because I didn't want them to. I suffered alone and just prayed that one day it would all go away. I may have looked to others as though I had it all together, but internally, I was a complete mess.

So if you take anything away from this chapter, I hope it will be to stop comparing yourself to others who walk in different shoes than you. Don't waste a single second of your day thinking less of yourself and your qualifications as a mother because someone else seems to have it all together, because again, no one really does. Just be true to who you are, and give yourself grace every single day. Accept that motherhood is beautiful but inevitably messy, and *don't gauge your happiness by how you think others see you. Caring too strongly about the opinions of others is a guaranteed recipe for a miserable life.* If you can just relax and accept that being a good mom isn't about being color-coordinated, having the cleanest car, or having perfectly obedient children, you may just get to experience a freedom and joy that you never have before.

Embracing Your God-Given Mommy Intuition

I have something to tell you that I hope brings you some encouragement. *You do NOT have to have this motherhood thing all figured out, and thinking that you do is the perfect recipe for anxiety, depression, and stress.* So let's not even go there, okay? Now, I'm writing this to myself as much as I am writing this to you because I started out as a mom, thinking that it was up to me to figure out how to do the "right" thing the "right" way at the "right" time for my child, and it freaked me out, to say the least.

I read every parenting book I could just, trying to get prepared for my baby's arrival, and I took notes and highlighted as if I was studying for the biggest exam of my life. What I didn't realize, though, is that God would give me the intuition and wisdom along the way and that I didn't need a manual. Now, don't get me wrong. I'm a big advocate for getting all the wisdom and advice you can as a parent, but ultimately, God will guide you if you ask Him to.

He will give you the intuition on when and how to introduce solids, how much screen time your kids should have, when to have "the talk," and so on. When I start doubting myself as a parent, I remind myself that my children were gifted to me and no one else because God knew that I would be the perfect parent for them.

Now, I don't mean "perfect" in the sense that you aren't allowed to ever mess up, lose your temper, or skip a beat, but I mean that God chose you and me because He knew we would be the parents that our unique child needed to have. God did not choose us by mistake, and it wasn't a coincidence! On those days that you may feel like a failure as a parent, give yourself grace, and remember that God's got your back. That "mommy gut" feeling everyone seems to talk about? Yeah, it's the real deal, and it's the Lord that gives it to you.

So pray daily, as I have learned to do, and ask God to give you the wisdom and intuition on how to parent your children, and then just roll with it. Take and read all the advice you want, but in the end, know that you don't have to have all the answers. Take a deep breath and allow God to guide you and know that you're doing an amazing job. Your mommy gut and the intuition God gives you will guide you even on days where you feel at your wit's end or unsure of what to do. Anxiety may creep in, and you may second guess yourself, but if you pray the simple prayer, "God, please help me know what to do," He *will* guide you.

I remember a couple of years ago, on a cold winter's night, when my one-year-old baby boy and I were wrapped up, sitting on the back porch stairs around 2 a.m. I had woken up to hearing him cough, but this cough to me seemed different. He sounded like he was croaking or as if he was barking like a dog. I went to check on him, and his lips seemed pale. I yelled to my husband, "Oh my gosh! He can't breathe!" This quickly brought me back to a few months prior when he was rushed to ER at around nine months old due to pneumonia, with a very high fever. It was like déjà vu all over again.

I quickly threw my coat on and wrapped him in a blanket and took him outside to breathe in the cold air, in hopes of opening his airway. At this time in my life, my anxiety was at an all-time high. Yet God gave me peace that night that my son was going to be okay and that I was doing the right thing. Instead of instantly dialing 911, God gave me the confidence and wisdom on how to care for my son. Then, the next day, I took him to the pediatrician for them to tell me, "It's just a croup cough." I put a humidifier in his room, and within a couple of days, he was fine.

A few months before this event, when we discovered he had pneumonia, I remember God just telling me to go to the ER right away. I remember waking my husband up and telling him to start the car while I put the baby in his carrier and ran next door to let my husband's grandmother know we were rushing out the door to the ER and leaving our three-year-old daughter asleep and in her care. At this time, we didn't know my son had pneumonia, but God just gave me that "mommy gut feeling" that my baby wasn't okay. Thank God we went when we did because his fever was nearing a hundred and five degrees by the time we got there. But God and the amazing ER staff took care of our baby boy, and a few days later, after being on a high dose of antibiotics, he was back to his happy, sweet self.

In a whole other nonmedical scenario, my daughter last year was in kindergarten at what was one of the best schools in the area. It was less than five minutes from our home, and it seemed like the perfect fit. Yet, a few months in, her spirit and overall demeanor changed, and she would beg me not to go. She was falling behind in reading, and she would ask me, "Why can't I read the way my friends can?"

My heart broke. I knew, at home, she had no problem recognizing words and reading to me, but it seemed that the second she walked into school, her confidence was gone. The teacher even mentioned to me that maybe she had a learning disability. That made me more discouraged and anxious than ever. I remember driving to my daughter's school and gripping the steering wheel on the way to pick her up after tutoring one day, ready to hear another discouraging update from her teacher, when it just hit me, "There is nothing wrong with her, but this is *not* the place for her."

I knew God was telling me this, and at first, it took some hard convincing on my part to get my husband on the same page, but eventually he agreed too. I was actually considering pulling her out for the remainder of the year, but then COVID hit, and before I knew it, the year was cut short, and I was my daughter's teacher.

It was a struggle, to say the least, as homeschooling is for sure *not* my calling (and I applaud every mommy who does do it because you are a freaking rock star), but she was home with me and away from a place that broke her spirit, and for that, I was grateful. This year she is in a new school that she loves and that she is thriving in, and I am so grateful. Despite what a perfect fit her school last year may have seemed to be, I know God gave me the intuition and wisdom to enroll her elsewhere, and I am so glad I listened.

So my message to you is this: regardless of what stage of parenting you are in, God is always waiting to guide you. Don't let Satan creep in and make you feel unqualified because you hit a few scary or discouraging bumps in the road. That is just how life goes. But God didn't give you this child or these children to care for alone. He knew you could do it *with* His help and guidance. All you have to do is pray daily for wisdom and then go with your gut feeling. Don't let Satan or anyone else scare you out of thinking that you know what is best for your child.

Read all of the parenting books you want, and take in all of the advice you can, but ultimately, trust that God will give you the intuition to do what is right for your child. So, confidently go with that, and let self-doubt fall by the wayside.

The Overwhelm

Do you want to know why some mornings you can't seem to get out of bed or find the willpower to take care of your children? Do you want to know why you find yourself with enormous guilt over the fact that you aren't able to enjoy motherhood as you always imagined you would? Many label this as "depression," but I believe that many times it's not that you're clinically depressed; it's that *you're actually just burnt out.* When you burn out, your brain shuts down, and your motivation goes out the window. Your body has been telling you that you're overtaxed, but you haven't been listening. You end up resenting your role as a mother, and sometimes even your kids. Then you end up snapping at them. Then the mom guilt kicks in. Then you feel like the worst mom on the planet. I'm sure you know what I am talking about. It's an awful, awful cycle, and one that I myself have had to be very careful to not get stuck in.

I've been in it many times before, and it's a miserable place to be. In order for me to be happy and peppy for my kids, I have to practice self-care, and I have to clock out for a few minutes every single day, no questions asked. I urge you to acknowledge that you need a break in order to be the best mom you can be. But here's the thing. A break isn't a break if you feel guilty the whole time. So, when you do take time for yourself each day, the key is to step away and *not to feel bad about it.* Your kids are fine. They can be left with your spouse, a family member, or a trusted babysitter for a few hours, a weekend, or even a week if needed. They won't be traumatized as I once thought. Honestly, depending on their age, they probably won't even remember.

These days, "Mommyyy!" is what is ringing in my ears from sunup to sundown, and truly, most of the time, I really, really love it. I love hearing them call my name, and I love being needed. Shoot, I waited six years to become a mother, so you better believe I appreciate it! But then sometimes, honestly, and as terrible as this may sound, I get burnt out, and I don't love being needed so much. Does this feeling sound familiar to you? Have you ever secretly wished you could change your name even for just an hour and disappear? I know I sure have!

But wait a minute. Shouldn't we embrace our role as mothers and be grateful for every second? Isn't it such a gift? It sure as heck is! However, I have news for you. *You're still human!* This whole "super mommy" meme is, well, garbage for lack of a better term. I hate to break it to you, but *when God made you a mother, He actually didn't give you supernatural powers,* and though He truly won't give us more than we can handle, we still will have hard days where we feel as if we are barely making it. We still will have days where we have to rely solely on Him just to make it through, and we still will have days that we wish *we* weren't relied on so heavily.

You are still *you,* and you still have physical and emotional needs. You are allowed to feel overwhelmed at times. Why, then, do we feel the need to hide the truth of how we are really feeling to our spouse, children, or ourselves when we are burnt out, sad, stressed, upset, or angry? Don't we teach our children to express themselves? So why, then, do we feel the need to paint on a smile day after day, to simply "play the part"? Why do we beat ourselves up when we get flustered or upset? Why can't we just own how we really feel?

Our children are always watching us. What are we teaching them when we are not true to ourselves and we are unwavering in our emotions? As much as I love being a mother, sometimes I still lose it. Sometimes I get irritated, short-tempered, or overwhelmed, and sometimes I end up having to apologize to my husband or kids. As much as I try day after day to be happy and chipper for my children, motherhood did not change the fact that I am still me. I still have moments and days where I get overwhelmed, and that is okay.

Here is a little blurb from my journal a few years back, right after my son was born, and I was left chasing a very rambunctious toddler, mostly alone, as my husband worked two jobs. I felt discouraged, overwhelmed, and so badly needing a moment to myself. It wasn't that I didn't love my children, but I also knew that I was in dire need of a mommy break, and I felt like I was screaming on the inside.

I wrote:

"So many emotions are going through me right now. I am just praying we can reach a happy normal soon. I am so blessed and grateful for all God

has given me, but sometimes I just wish I had more time to breathe. I need to pray for more wisdom on how to obtain that. Chris and I haven't had a date in a while, and my hormones are all over the place. Life is just so crazy, and I just feel like I can't keep up."

Clearly I was desperate for a few moments to just collect my thoughts and to step away. If I remember correctly, after I wrote this, I found myself at Starbucks alone for a couple hours because I ended up crying to my husband when he came home from work that I was about to "lose my crap."

Listen, it is okay to not be okay, Mama. It is okay to feel that you need a break, and it is okay that you don't want to do this mom thing twenty-four-seven. Again, I will remind you that you are human, and everyone deserves a break, including you. So, take a step back when you feel that you are about to burst on the inside. Or better yet, take one *before* you get to that point and without an ounce of guilt.

No one can constantly run the marathon of motherhood and never stop to breathe. So when you feel that feeling of claustrophobia and overwhelm creeping in, then step away. I promise you will be glad you did, and you will be happily ready to conquer whatever comes your way when you return.

Recognizing the Signs of PPD and PPA

Five years. It took me five years into my motherhood career and a national pandemic to admit to my husband how badly I had been really suffering. I was ashamed and afraid that he would think me incapable of taking care of our children if I let on how emotionally distraught I had been.

He recently grabbed my hand over breakfast on our anniversary weekend getaway when I found myself getting emotional talking about the past and how I had silently suffered. I told him just how overwhelmingly grateful I felt to just feel how I was feeling then. I told him how free and happy I felt and how long it had really been since I felt that way. Then he grabbed my hand across the table and said, "I am so sorry you felt that you couldn't tell me, and I am sorry you suffered this way for so long. If I could, I would go back in time and help you through it." But, he didn't know because I didn't tell him. Thankfully, now our marriage is in the best place it has ever been, all thanks to God and our hard work on communication, and now he knows what I went through. Now, my secret is out of the bag, and I finally have found healing. But it wasn't easy getting here.

So anyway, now I am on a little white pill called "Lexapro." Yup, I am a holistic, tree-hugging health junkie who went on an anything-but-natural antidepressant, and you know what? I am so unbelievably glad that I did. I started Lexapro at the start of the pandemic. I was going at such a healthy pace in life, and then, boom! Life was flipped upside down. It's no secret to my loved ones that this mama just needs space sometimes, and during the pandemic, I was just unable to get it. I am sure most of you know what I mean and can relate. I honestly felt as I couldn't get space to save my life, and I also was responsible for homeschooling my daughter, which I had never done before. Some amazing moms out there are cut out for homeschooling, and I admire them so much, but I am not one of those moms. I'm just not.

The truth is, though, I should have started on Lexapro six years ago, after my daughter was born. But I didn't because I was fine, right? I mean, isn't a mom supposed to be emotional and feel like a freak of nature for a while? Survival mode is a mom's reality, isn't it? To a point, yes, but this should not go on forever, and if you feel as if you are drowning and you are past the six-month postpartum stage, then I advise you to really sit down and evaluate how you are feeling. Did you know that women can suffer from PPD and/or PPA (postpartum depression and postpartum anxiety) for years? Some women have even been reported being diagnosed fifteen years after their youngest child was born! It is a dark spiral that can keep going if not properly treated and recognized.

Here are some major postpartum depression and anxiety symptoms to look out for after you have had your baby and sometimes even years down the road:

- Guilt
- Anger

- Sadness
- Anxiety about being left alone
- Extreme worry for the well-being of your child
- Thoughts of suicide
- Images of hurting your baby
- Insomnia
- Changes in your appetite
- Feeling numb and disconnected
- Being unable to enjoy activities you once did
- Lack of motivation
- Feeling hopeless
- Feeling unqualified to be a mother
- Palpitations or feeling as if your heart is racing
- Extreme fatigue
- Lack of desire to have sex.

...and the list goes on and on. Needless to say, PPD and PPA are not pretty, and I would not wish them on anyone. Leading up to me finally getting the help I needed, I was in a very dark place. I cannot begin to imagine where I would have been if I had not been so diligent in caring for my health as I was throughout that time. Honestly, if I hadn't, I don't know if I could have functioned.

So, my message to you is this: *don't suffer alone,* and be on the lookout for any of these symptoms that you may experience. Again, even if your youngest child is a few years old, it is still not unheard of for a woman to be still suffering from PPD or PPA. Once the chemicals in your brain have been knocked off-kilter, it can take a very long time, and often, medical intervention, for them to normalize. So talk to your husband, talk to your friends and family, and then I urge you to talk to your doctor. It's not to say that you will end up needing medication as I did, but if you do, I want you to know that it is not the end of the world. In fact, it just may be the missing key that allows you to really start living your life again.

Please don't wait to get help. Every day is such a gift, so don't waste a single moment being stuck in the same agony that I was. There is so much holistic and modern medicine available to help you! I hope you choose to love yourself enough and take advantage of it and also to talk to your loved ones about how you are struggling. I can promise if you do, you won't regret it.

The World Was Already Spinning

I don't think that anyone could have prepared me for the feeling of holding my baby for the very first time. After trying to have a child for a few years, it just seemed surreal to me that I was no longer just the aunt or the babysitter and that I was finally the "mommy." In a sense, my world seemed to stand still. When they first laid my daughter on my chest, it was as if I was dreaming or almost having an out-of-body experience. It just didn't seem real, and my life as I knew it from that moment on forever changed. I finally was given the privilege and opportunity to care, love, and raise a little person that I could call my own.

Before I knew it, this little one was the center of my existence. I was changing her diapers and nursing her by day and then doing it all over again by night. My life revolved around my baby girl, it seemed, and I felt as though everything else I once knew became a blur and no longer mattered as much as it once did. My every moment seemed to revolve around her, my precious baby girl with the longest eyelashes and fullest head of black hair I had ever seen.

The harsh reality was, though, that regardless of how much my life had changed, life around me still kept going. As much as I wanted to stay in my own little world and just sit at home and nurse on the couch, duty called. I quickly realized that life was not going to slow down just because I had a baby. This sparked a feeling of anxiety in me because I didn't feel confident tackling both life as I knew it and my new life with my baby, combined. What I know now that I so wish I had known then is that *it wasn't up to me to fit into her world, but instead it was up to me to help her fit into ours.*

As much as I wanted to just sit on the couch and snuggle my baby all day, the reality was that after those first precious few weeks were over, I couldn't. I still had things to do, people to see, and places to be. I still needed to eat, sleep, and shower, even if the latter was spent rushing as I listened to my baby cry for me (even though she had already been changed and fed).

I still was trying to stay in touch with my clients and put in some hours in the office as they had not yet found a replacement for me. Then, once they finally did find a replacement for me, the training process began. This all went on for months—me at the front desk, working as a receptionist with my baby girl tucked away in her carrier, sleeping under my desk. Now, let me tell you, bringing a tiny baby to work in an infant carrier to sit under your desk while you answer calls is NOT something I would advise anyone. It was horrific. However, ironically enough, I was grateful that I was called back into work so soon because it forced me to maintain some sort of structure in my life that, at the time, seemed to be anything *but* structured.

The thing is, I felt guilty about having to go back to work even though my daughter was with me. I felt guilty because I could no longer give my baby girl all of my attention. I felt pulled in so many directions, and I felt guilty that I could not give each area of my life my all. Mostly, though, I felt guilty that my daughter's life was not as structured as I had imagined it would be or as I had read about how an infant's life "should" have been. The schedule I had typed up to follow for her went out the window, and I found myself taking each day hour by hour.

I had imagined, while pregnant, me at home most of the day, just staring at my new baby and soaking up her cuteness as people came to visit and bring us meals. Thankfully, that actually was the reality for the first few weeks, until one day it wasn't, and reality sank in. As soon as life got going again, I still tried my hardest to ensure I was home as much as possible for my daughter's sake, because that's what a baby needs, right? I had read so many times, "A baby needs structure." So I wanted to put her down in her crib for each nap and keep her home, in a germ-safe environment, as much as I could. But that just didn't seem to happen every day like I wanted.

After six weeks were up, my job needed me. The replacement they originally had for me fell through, and they needed me to step in. It ultimately was up to me to choose to go back to work or not, but I knew I had to go back to at least help them out until they found someone to take over my job. So I packed my tiny baby up each morning, day after day, and I ventured into the work world.

On top of those first few months of work, I also had errands to run and things to do. I just couldn't avoid my to-do list forever and not get anything done.

Sitting at home all day just wasn't an option, and I quickly discovered that it wasn't mentally healthy for me. Thankfully, and despite my guilt, after the first few months, I figured out that I could easily nurse my daughter and change her in the car, take her grocery shopping and to postpartum follow-ups, and for the most part, do what I needed to do. I realized that structure and being home all day sounded nice on paper, but for me, it just wasn't doable, or at least not every day.

As time went on, I started to pick up on my daughter's cues, and I started to pinpoint her fussier times and the times that were best to be out and about. So I did schedule around that the best I could. However, I learned that for me, being productive was a huge boost for my overall mood, and so I knew that I couldn't just sit at home all day. Even on days where I was able to stay at home all day, I still would take her for a walk around a neighborhood nearby, just to get out of the house and see other faces. Staying within four walls all day, just me, the TV, and my baby just simply wasn't healthy for me. The days that I did end up staying home all day, I noticed that my depression and anxiety would be at their worst. Thankfully, today, if we are snowed in, for example, I am able to be home for days at a time without suffering any blues, but that unfortunately was not the case for me at that time in my life.

So even once my work found a new replacement for me, and I no longer was needed, I still kept making it a point to leave the house to do at least one productive thing each day. The problem was that I still felt guilt creep in for leaving the house if it meant that the schedule I tried so hard to maintain for my baby got disrupted. That is, until one day when I read a certain quote. I honestly can't remember the whole quote or where I even saw it, but the gist of it was: *"Regardless of what changes take place in your life, the world will keep on spinning as it did before."*

Then it hit me. Yes, my daughter was now here, but she was born into an already spinning world. I couldn't just stop the world from spinning, and I couldn't completely stop living my life just to fit into hers. Instead, it was *my* job to teach her how to adapt to our life and fit into this big and crazy world. It was okay that I kept going and that life wasn't all about her. It was okay that I still had a desire to still use my gifts and consult with my clients. God had given me a gift to help others and a passion for health, and I didn't want to let either go. Scarlett, of course, remained at the top of my priority list. But still, other things and people needed me, and I realized that was okay.

Now, listen. I really am a huge advocate for schedules and routines, and I made many necessary adjustments along the way for my new baby, but after reading that quote, I felt that God had spoken to me to let me know that it was okay that I kept carrying on with life. *As much as most mothers, including myself, wish time would just stand still, it doesn't.* So, I unapologetically gave myself permission to keep on going.

Now, I didn't keep going because I always *wanted* to, but because I knew I had to. Honestly, with PPD and PPA, some days I wanted nothing more than to shut the blinds and stay in bed all day. Yet, the demands of life kept me going.

My daughter was still at the top of my list, but she wasn't the *only* thing on my list. The reality was that I still had other things to attend to. It's just how it was. Now, looking back, I understand why I felt the guilt I did. I was on the go quite a bit in my daughter's first year of life, and it really was chaotic at times. It also wasn't anything like I had pictured it would be. Also, if you remember, my husband was working two jobs and building our home on top of it, so we really didn't have very much of the quality family time I hoped for either. Nothing was perfect or going as I imagined it would. However, I know that despite my circumstances, I did the best I could, which is all any of us are expected to do.

So I am writing all of this to say that if you are anxiously wondering, as I was, how in the heck you will be able to manage caring for an infant well and keeping up with all the demands of life, remember this: *God is bringing your baby into an already-spinning world, and He already has all of the variables worked out. Despite the chaos that your life brings, God gave your baby the ability to adapt, and he or she will be just fine.* So, take a deep breath, Mama, and try not to stress the little things. It will all work out, I promise.

Really, once your baby is born, he or she is just along for the ride. So don't beat yourself up because you have other responsibilities on your plate. *Your baby can still be the apple of your eye even if you are a busy mom on the go. You don't need to feel guilty for getting back into the swing of life.* Listen, my schedule was anything but ideal in my daughter Scarlett's first year of life, but today, she is a happy and healthy child with no memories of the chaos that occurred, and she is perfectly fine. Heck, to be honest, life never has slowed down for me! If anything, as time has gone on, it has gotten even busier and crazier. Yet, I can confidently say that both of my children are well-rounded, healthy, happy, and loved. So, I guess I must be doing okay.

If you are reading this and you are feeling stuck in the same crazy boat as I was and are being pulled in a million different directions, then I want to encourage you once more that your baby or your children will be fine, and they will adapt even when life gets hectic. Truthfully, I don't believe there is a "perfect schedule" for an infant or child anyway if you ask me. So do yourself a favor and throw that thought straight out the window. Babies and children are all so different, so as a mother, you will find that studying them is very important. The more you do, the more you will discover what they need and when.

Now, if you are blessed enough to not work and stay home with nothing to do but care for your house and child or children, then that is wonderful and seriously such a gift! Trust me, I know how much work staying at home is, and I applaud you for it! However, if you *are* working or needing to go back to work or attend to other responsibilities outside of the home, then know that that is okay too.

What I personally have discovered as a mother is that flexible children are happier children. Now, don't get me wrong. As I keep saying, I am all for nap times in the crib and meals at home in the high chair when possible. However, this is just not always doable, and that is okay. In fact, if you ask me, changing things up and teaching your children from a young age to be flexible is one of the best ways to help prepare them for the changes that will come later on in life when they are older. *Also, children and babies are WAY more adaptable and resilient than we give them credit for!* So keep that in mind when leaving the house with your little one in tow.

Of course, always follow your mommy intuition, but also remind yourself that it's okay to venture out, even if it throws a wrench in the schedule from time to time. Let your baby nap and eat on the go if needed, and do yourself a favor and save yourself the guilt trip. Our babies were born into a world that was already spinning. So, do your best to teach them how to adapt to it, and don't feel the need to put life on hold for so long. Just set the guilt aside, ask God for wisdom and discernment, and then keep chugging along. You've got this, Mama!

Mommy Guilt at Its Finest

You caught me red-handed, and to tell you the truth, I didn't even plan on writing this chapter, but the last two days' events convinced me that I had to. With every trial or trying day comes a lesson or something to be learned, and so I'm going to swallow my pride, make the time to squeeze in an extra writing session, and not skip over this one.

Okay, so I guess I will start by telling you that I've been a cranky mess for two days, and I spent the majority of the morning snapping at my children and on the brink of tears. To just put it all out on the table, my visit from "Aunt Flo" is due at any second, and I just feel like a rubber band that finally has been pulled to its limit and snapped. Have you ever felt this way? I know most can agree they have and that it downright sucks to feel like you've lost your cool on your kids, especially when you are about to leave town. But today, I did.

Before having my daughter, I was determined to be a mom who was cool, calm, and collected. I thought, "If Michelle Duggar with her nineteen kids can claim to never raise her voice to her children, then why can't I?" But, sometimes I do cry, yell, and wish I could lock myself away. Look, I truly applaud Michelle Duggar for her patience, and I look up to her so much, but I am not always able to say that I deal with each parenting situation calmly. "My grace is sufficient for you," God says, and thank God for that, because I would be lost without it.

So anyway, moving on, I just spent the last few minutes apologizing to my kids for raising my voice and explaining to them why Mommy was so upset. As a side note, I will say that I think it's very import-ant and healthy to teach our children that it is okay to express their emotions in a healthy way and to let them be heard. Raising my voice is something I really try hard to never do. But again, I'm human and imper-fect, and sometimes it happens.

When I do lose it, though, I make it a point to always try and apologize shortly afterward. I then try my best to explain my feelings and emotions to my kids. When I explain my hurt and anger to them and vice versa, it builds our bond and understanding of one another. They want to be heard, and so do I. It may be in my "right" as a parent to simply give my kids instruction and just declare to them it's "because I said so." But I've learned that when I don't explain myself and just demand their obedience, I lose their heart, and our connection is tampered with.

Okay, so back to me losing my temper this morning, or should I say originally last night. First, allow me to set the scene for you. It's the week after Christmas, and only a couple of days before my husband and I venture off to the beautiful beaches of Cancun for my brother's destination wedding that has been in the works for two years. I have spent days cleaning and organizing the kids' new Christmas toys into bins stacked neatly on shelves, doing endless amounts of laundry, and cleaning the house from top to bottom. Leaving the house in order always gives me the mental clarity I need to go on vacation and really relax, so I always make a point to get it done. Adding all of the holiday hustle and cleanup to the mix added a bit of stress, but I knew all of my hard work would be well worth it once I was finished. Physical clutter has always stressed me out, so I try my hardest, especially after Christmas, to organize the new toys the best I can.

Anyway, last night, after all the cleaning was finished, my husband and I decided to finish tackling our packing lists and suitcases, and so we let our kids stay up a little late and play in the living room until we finished. Thirty minutes had passed when I went to go check on the kids. What I saw in the living room was enough to make me have a panic attack, cry, scream, and just want to go hide under my bed covers.

Every. Single. Toy I had spent the last two days organizing into neat little bins with lids was dumped into the living room floor in one big, jumbled mess. I couldn't believe my eyes. "What did you guys just do?!?!" I yelled at the top of my lungs. They both innocently looked at me and then each other and casually answered, "Oh, we were playing store." I then walked out of the room, back to my husband, almost shaking. I couldn't believe how much work they had just undone. I told my husband I was too angry to calmly speak to them about the disaster they had just made, so he went and talked to them, and over the next hour, he directed them on cleaning it up.

After a few minutes, I had calmed myself enough to quickly rush through their bedtime routine, kiss them, and say good night. But I was still so upset. The toys were "put away," but far from how organized I had originally had them, and I still felt so frustrated at my kids. Yet, I decided to move on, and I decided to just start fresh the next day, as hard as that was.

So fast-forward to this morning when I lost my temper...again. It's the day before our departure, and I just sent both kids outside to play on their play set for a few minutes while I finished cleaning up the kitchen and mopping the floors. (Side note: nothing makes me happier than sparkling-clean floors to come back to after a trip). Anyway, not even a minute or two after I finished mopping, both kids ran inside with their boots caked in mud and proceeded to run in circles and chase each other, leaving the floor covered in clumps of mud and grass. I found myself one step forward and five steps back, and once again, I wanted to cry. "What were you guys thinking, running in here without removing your shoes at the door?! Look at the mess you guys just made for Mommy to clean up!" I felt so incredibly frustrated and disrespected.

Let me play the devil's advocate for a minute and just say that though my kids generally know I prefer that they remove their shoes when they come inside, they are also little, and I know they easily can forget. Not to mention I had been the one who sent them outside to play without taking account of the mud due to yesterday's rain, so honestly, it was partially my fault. Yet, I still was so frustrated by all of the work that had just been undone yet again.

We were about to leave for an adults' only trip, and yet here I was, just this morning, snapping at my kids, who I won't see for a week? I felt like a crap parent after the fact, and I was disappointed in myself for freaking out on them just before leaving when I had pictured nothing but fun times and sweet snuggles. But this morning (and last night) was just another reminder to me that it's by God's grace alone that I am able to do this parenting thing and make it through each day. *Parenting is an incredibly fulfilling yet draining job at the same time that requires both the receiving and the giving of grace.*

So here I sit on an early morning flight to Cancun, already missing my babies, and I'm wrapping up this chapter with the reminder to both you and me to extend grace to our kids and to ourselves every single day. Parenting is no walk in the park, and sometimes we will get frustrated and not handle situations as calmly as we should. But, there is always grace available for us, and Lord willing, another day to rise again and start over.

So try and shake off the frustration, wipe off those tears, direct the kids in cleaning up the mud or whatever mess they made, and know that everything is going to be okay. Your kids still know that you love them, even on your worst days, and even when you lose your temper, so don't be too hard on yourself, okay? I bet you aren't still upset over the temper tantrum your toddler threw this morning at breakfast, are you? So why still be upset and dwell on yours? Apologize to your babies, hug it out, and then just move on. I promise you, no permanent damage has been done, so try not to beat yourself up too much. Reject the mommy guilt, and remember that God's grace is sufficient, and tomorrow is another day.

Pinpointing Your Triggers

We all have things that set us off. Maybe it's something linked back to a traumatic experience from your
childhood; maybe it's linked to something that happened to you as an adult; or maybe it's not linked to
a personal experience at all. Maybe it is a person, a
place, or even a song. Whatever or whoever it is, it is a
trigger for you if it manifests into anxiety, steals your
joy, and keeps you from living and enjoying your life.

For me, and as long as I can remember, my triggers have revolved around the topic of health. It may
be because I grew up with both my parents being in
the medical field, or maybe it was due to the fact that
I had to go through two major surgeries to correct my
severe scoliosis at the young age of twelve (that also
required me to wear a back brace and hardly move for
an entire year). It also could have been partly due and
made worse by my struggle to stay pregnant and the
five losses I experienced before my two miracle babies
were born.

To tell you the truth, though, I don't really know
the exact reason as to why my stomach gets bunched
into knots when I walk into a doctor's office or why
I always jump to thinking something awful like cancer is the reason behind my child's cold symptoms,
bruises, or fatigue. But the reality is, I would easily
take skydiving over taking myself or anyone I love to
the doctor and having to wait for test results of some
sort. My mind always thinks, "This is it. Something

terrible and life-altering is going to show up in those results." Yes, this is really how my brain spirals out of control and thinks at times. Thankfully, through lots of self-care, holistic medicine, and Lexapro, I have come a long way, but truthfully, I still struggle.

So what have I learned to do? *I've learned to not set myself up for extra opportunities to be triggered.* Some things like taking my kids to the doctor are unavoidable, but some things are, like browsing Dr. Google, watching medical shows like *Grey's Anatomy*, and clicking on a St. Jude's ad to learn more about the child in the picture. It's not that I'm heartless to no longer read up on these children, and it's not that I desire to live under a rock. I avoid these scenarios because my mind doesn't stop after the story ends. I immediately want to know more about the specific form of cancer the child has or had and what that child's first symptom was that the parents first noticed. Then I start over-evaluating my kids' every little cough and sniffle, then poof! Just like that, my peace and joy are gone.

Maybe this medical anxiety I am describing is totally foreign to you. Truthfully, I really hope it is because I would not wish this anxiety on even my worst enemy. It can be absolutely debilitating.

However, even if you can't relate to my medical anxiety, I bet you can pinpoint at least one thing that triggers you and leaves you feeling anxious and stripped of peace and joy. Think on it for a minute if you have to, and then answer me this: what do you do to protect yourself from it? We have, on average, sixteen hours in a twenty-four-hour period that we are typically awake in our day, and yet it can take only thirty seconds or less to see or read something that leaves us in a pit the rest of the day. Again, it doesn't have to be a certain "thing," but maybe it is a toxic "someone" in your life that, whenever you see them, you instantly feel drained, anxious, or depressed.

Whatever or whoever it is, it is up to us to protect our hearts and our minds from it or them as much as possible, so that we can then live our best life, being fully present with those we love, instead of being trapped living in a pit of anxiety and unrest. Triggers will inevitably pop up in our lives, but if there is a way to avoid them, then we should. God will help us sort through our anxious thoughts and give us peace in life if we ask Him, but it is up to us to protect our mental headspace and not put ourselves in the line of fire.

Clocking out to Focus on Your Marriage

Healthy relationships are essential for our mental health, happiness, and quality of life. Our marriage especially, is a relationship that we must value, nurture and protect. A healthy marriage takes intention and it takes time, time spent alone that is. The truth is that I used to be extremely against leaving my kids. In fact, when my daughter was fifteen months old, my husband wanted to take me on a weekend getaway and I told him if we went, she would have to come. I just wasn't ready to leave her. Fast-forward fifteen minutes into our arrival, when my little toddler made a beeline straight for the toilet. Within seconds, my husband and I heard a splash and an "uh-oh," and we quickly hurried to the bathroom to discover her one and only sippy cup we brought for the weekend in the toilet. This started off a trend on what was supposed to be a trip just for us. Instead of reconnecting and having time for us, we ended up chasing a very rambunctious, adorable toddler throughout a resort all weekend, looking for ways to entertain her.

It was after that vacation that quickly became a "trip" that I realized I had to let go of my mommy guilt and take time away from our daughter to work on our marriage. It's not that we were in a bad place, but if I am being honest, we weren't great. We were trying to navigate parenthood, our new home, and both of our new roles. I was now a stay-at-home, working mom, and my husband had just started his new job.

We so needed time for us, and I knew that it was up to me to make it happen. Shortly after we got back, we committed to every-other-week date nights, and a few months later we went back to the resort and had the most amazing and relaxing time together, just the two of us.

The grass is greener where you water it, and I realized that I had to get back to putting my husband and marriage first, as God intends it to be. I had to start making a conscious effort to spend time with my husband and step away from my role as a mom once in a while. We decided we wanted to start dating each other again. So, we did. We reconnected, and ultimately we were better parents for our daughter as we finally felt back on the same page.

Do you want to know what's crazy though? As soon as my husband and I started to take time for us again and I had finally come to terms with the fact that I didn't need to feel guilty about it, the mom-shaming started. I wasn't shamed by everyone. Most family and friends were supportive, but some were not. I heard comments like, "Wow, you guys go on a lot of dates" or "Oh, I could never leave my child overnight that young." Though these individuals may have meant well, it honestly really hurt me. I was trying so hard to balance the juggling act of marriage, parenting, and work, and I felt like I finally had a good handle on it. So then, when I was told that I had gotten it all wrong, it really stung. You know what though? We decided to keep doing what we were doing. I decided that my marriage and sanity mattered more to me than those people's opinions, and I wasn't going to listen.

That was nearly five years ago now. Fast-forward to us today with two kids in tow and I can still happily report that we still date each other and go on trips and we are better for it. We have been married for thirteen years, and we are doing better than we ever have. But we have had to work at it. It hasn't always come easy. We had to intentionally take time back for us and take time away from parenting to nurture our marriage and ultimately be better parents for our kids in the end. Our happy marriage wasn't just handed to us. It took, and still takes, lots of work and dedication, but man, has it been worth it! I hope that you, too, will step away from your kids for a time and devote time solely to your spouse on a routine basis. If you do, I can promise that you will not only richly bless you and your husband but your children as well. So, don't wait. Start dating your spouse again *today.*

When Mama Is All Touched Out

Let's talk about sex for a second, shall we? Yup, you heard me right. Let's talk about s-e-x because it's a big freaking deal and a very important part of marriage. Now, if it's not something you are comfortable talking about, then no worries! Sit back, relax, and I will do all of the talking.

Okay, so let's cut straight to the chase. It's no secret that oftentimes, moms just feel *all touched out*. I know I myself have inwardly screamed multiple times to my kids and my husband, "Please, just get your hands off me for two freaking seconds!" From the moment we get pregnant, our body is constantly changing and shifting to make room for our growing baby, and some days we just don't feel so hot. Even three years out from giving birth, I can vouch that some days I still feel the same way, and I just don't want to be touched. It's not that I don't love and desire to be intimate with my husband, but some days I struggle with feeling overtaxed and overstimulated, and sex is frankly the last thing on my mind.

Motherhood in itself is beautiful and so rewarding, but sometimes, when hormones and extra pounds are thrown in, we may not feel that way. While pregnant and as a mother, you will have days that you feel beautiful and glowing, and then you will have days when you feel like just hiding under the covers all day. Again, as frustrating as our up-and-down emotions may be, it is normal to feel this way. First we have our baby, then we move on to the nursing stage, then the clingy toddler stage, and then the preschool melt-down, cling-to-your-leg stage, and then, well...you get the picture.

I know for me, personally, starting off, I was very self-conscious the first few months of my pregnancy with my daughter because I didn't look pregnant yet, but nothing fit. In fact, I didn't have that cute "basket-ball tummy" I had always imagined until I hit about twenty weeks. Not to mention, my breasts hurt so bad that I even dreaded taking my bra on or off. I also, as you now know, had suffered multiple miscarriages, and I unfortunately had a bleeding episode with my daughter's pregnancy in the first trimester (that thankfully turned out to be nothing) that left me on edge.

So all of this to say, with my poor body image and paranoia at an all-time high, do you think I was in the "mood" for sex? I am sure you can guess the answer to that question. The answer was *no.* I was tired, ner-vous, and always checking for blood each time I went to the bathroom. The last thing I wanted to do was risk another bleeding episode by having sex. I didn't feel like myself, and honestly, I just didn't want to be touched. Ironically, in the third trimester, when my belly was at its biggest, my "mojo" came back for a couple of months, only to vanish again once the baby was born.

Am I telling you all of this to discourage you or scare you if you are a soon-to-be mother? Absolutely not. But I wish someone had told it to me straight and prepared me a little bit more for how I might feel about sex during pregnancy and in my early stages of motherhood so that maybe I wouldn't feel so guilty. Sadly, though, the truth is that during this time in my life, I hurt my husband's feelings a lot. *I never really communicated to him how I was feeling about my body and about the pregnancy. All he really knew was my constant rejection.* I wasn't harsh towards him, and I tried to be kind about it, yet I still didn't help him really understand. We really had had a pretty amazing sex life up until I found out I was pregnant, but then I flipped the tables on him. I felt so incredibly different, yet he didn't, and his needs hadn't changed.

Now, jump ahead to my pregnancy with my son, when I felt more prepared and less like a deer in the headlights. This time around, I was able to better help my husband understand how I was feeling, and so he took less offense to it. I'll be blunt with you and tell you that I still didn't have much of a sexual drive, but after several heart-to-heart conversations, I realized that he just couldn't "deal with it" and go without and that it wasn't right for me to expect him to. So, I ahem... "helped him out" and made sure he was taken care of two to three times a week.

Side note: coconut oil works wonderfully as an all-natural lubricant. Oh whoops, was that TMI? Well, ladies, I didn't write this book to mumble my words. Sex during pregnancy and during the early stages of motherhood is often a topic that is just not discussed, yet it is a constant struggle and strain in so many relationships. It's the big elephant in the room, so let's stop being hush-hush about it, shall we?

The reality is that God created sex in a marriage as an act of love and devotion. I once heard that it allows God in, and it keeps Satan out. It strengthens your connection in every way, physically, emotionally, and spiritually. It is incredibly important, and there is a reason they call it "make-up sex"! I once heard our pastor describe it as "the healing balm within a marriage." Sex is *not* just for making babies; it is designed by God to be enjoyable and to keep us close. It allows us to be vulnerable and totally open with our husbands in a way that we aren't with anyone else.

Okay, so now that we have established how vital it is, what is a tired, stressed-out mama to do? If sex is SO great, then why do we not desire it all of the time like our husbands do? Why don't we share their same drive? Well, it is due to a combination of things, but if I had to narrow it down, I would argue that it is mainly due to our *hormones.* Let's think about this from a scientific standpoint. If we choose to or are able to breastfeed, our estrogen and progesterone are suppressed, and our prolactin is elevated, which has been shown in many studies to leave our libido in the trash.

But breastfeeding aside, motherhood in general can easily put a damper on it. Why? Well, again, over-stimulation and being touched all day does not do anything to help a woman relax. Our stress hormone cortisol is through the roof, and we can hardly find a second to slow down. We are so busy trying to care for our babies that we can't even think straight some days, much less think about sex. Yet, we are stuck feeling guilty because we feel as if we are letting our husbands down. In the meantime, our husbands don't have to go through the physical changes we do, and their testosterone just keeps steadily pumping. It just doesn't seem fair, does it? Yet, when Adam and Eve sinned, God gave men and women different burdens to bear.

Now, look, I get it. We just want to feel as we did once before. We want to have sensual thoughts towards our husbands, but we just can't get there. If you are feeling this way, I want you to know that I 1000 percent understand where you are coming from. But hear me out when I tell you that there is hope. Today, I can proudly say that we have a very healthy sex life once again and that we both genuinely desire each other. However, getting back to this point took some work. Thankfully, now I think I have it down to a science of what works to balance my hormones and keep my libido in check.

Here are my top tips to get your "mojo" back and enjoy time between the sheets once again with your husband:

- Try Emerita progesterone cream to balance your hormones (if your doctor approves, of course). This works wonders!
- Ask your husband to help you relax so that you can mentally "get there." Maybe this means

for him to put the kids to bed or give you a massage. You know what relaxes you, so you fill in the blank.

- Communicate, communicate, communicate! Your husband loves you, and as much as I am sure he would like to, he actually doesn't understand how you feel. So lovingly communicate to him how you are feeling physically and mentally, and help him to better understand versus leaving him to just figure you out.
- Ask him to take you out on a date! Nothing turns a tired mama on more than dressing up and going out with her hubby to eat good food (that she didn't have to cook) and spending time alone with her husband *without* kids yelling in the background. Can I get an amen! In our book, on date nights, sex is just a given, and we always look forward to it and know it's coming. By the time we get home, we just spent the last couple of hours connecting, so we are ready to go! But again, even still three years out from having our son, I still wouldn't be able to mentally and physically "get there" if I hadn't had that break and time to communicate with my husband *first.* Most men can easily jump to intimacy without much of a conversation first, but women desire to be emotionally taken care of ahead of time. If you feel that you can't afford to eat out, then go have a picnic. All that matters is that you are together reconnecting!

- Consider asking your doctor about the supplement P5P, which is a broken-down form of vitamin B6. It is easily metabolized, and it works wonders in restoring hormone balance and libido! Twenty-five milligrams a day was my go-to for the first year or so after each of my babies was born. It also helps to increase your energy and stabilize your mood. It's incredible!

Now keep in mind that in our marriage, our sex life can easily sizzle out even when we are far out of the baby stage and thriving in all other areas. We can so easily get so tied up in life, and we can lose sight of other aspects that matter. When this happens, we end up coexisting like roommates, and that is not healthy. So, what my husband and I have found is that even when life is crazy, if we are intentional about having sex often, then our communication is better. On the flip side, if we are intentional about taking time to date each other and communicate, then our sex life is better. They are all interconnected.

I have been married for thirteen years (yup, I was a baby when I got married at the ripe age of eighteen), and though I am no expert, I know this to be true. We have gone through many "dry spells" in our marriage, and I can tell you firsthand that it affected every other area. Also, my husband has let me know on countless occasions how much our sex life means to him and how much it makes him feel loved. Clearly it's a big deal, and I can vouch that on behalf of our marriage, when we make intimacy a priority, even when one of us doesn't initially feel like it, it is a huge game-changer!

So I guess if I could leave you with one thing that marriage as a whole has taught me, it would be this: *it is up to US as a couple to both be intentional in our marriage and to keep the flame of love and passion burning strong so that Satan doesn't have a chance to creep in.* So communicate, work as a team, have fun together, and when all else fails...Netflix and chill.

The Beauty of Genuine Friendships

I recently read an article written by Meghan Markle in the *New York Times,* where she announced her recent miscarriage. She also went on to talk about a time the year prior when she was in South Africa with her husband and new son. She wrote,

"I recalled a moment last year when Harry and I were finishing up a long tour in South Africa. I was exhausted. I was breastfeeding our infant son, and I was trying to keep a brave face in the very public eye. "Are you OK?" a journalist asked me. I answered him honestly, not knowing that what I said would resonate with so many—new moms and older ones, and anyone who had, in their own way, been silently suffering. My off-the-cuff reply seemed to give people permission to speak their truth. But it wasn't responding honestly that helped me most; it was the question itself. "Thank you for asking," I said. "Not many people have asked if I'm OK."

This article really resonated with me because I think so many of us get so busy that we end up coexisting with one another. We often get so busy that before we know it, it's been weeks since we have checked in with our friends. Or maybe you are one of those people that does check in on your girlfriends, yet deep down, you feel hurt because you don't feel as if anyone ever checks in on you. "Are you okay?" "How is life treating you?" "What's new with you?"

As women and mothers, especially, we crave community, and these are the questions, I believe, that we all long to be asked. Motherhood can be very isolating, scary, and overwhelming at every stage, and we need to stick together and have friends that check in on us, support us, and love us through the good times and the bad.

I remember around my thirtieth birthday last year, when it really hit me. I am the one who does a lot of the pursuing in most of my relationships. It's just who I am, and I am usually okay with it. It all comes down to the fact that I simply long for closeness and companionship, and as a result, I naturally fall into a pattern of doing 90 percent of the work in my relationships to keep connections strong. I am "that girl" that typically sends out a text or puts in a call to her close friends and family at least once a week, just to catch up and see how they are doing.

I am and have always been a social butterfly, and relationships have always been extremely important to me, so naturally, I have always been one to put a lot of effort into them. This hasn't always been easy, as most of my close friends and I have all gone on to get married and have families of our own and are seemingly busier and busier every year that passes. But yet, I have always kept them as a high priority because I believe that community is so incredibly important (especially as moms).

I noticed last year, though, after I had experienced a hard few months with some extended family members, that I was left feeling depleted and deeply hurt, and I felt as if I had less emotionally to give to others, which led me to that yucky feeling of guilt. I wanted to be there for those I loved, as I always had strived to be, but inwardly I felt empty and sad. I needed someone to check in on *me* and ask me, "Are you okay?"

These emotional few months brought me to the realization that I had a few one-sided relationships in my life that were draining me dry. I realized that in a few relationships that I had labeled as "friendships," I was the only one reaching out and checking in on them and extending the invitations for playdates or a girls' night. Yet, it wasn't reciprocated. Now, this is in no way meant as a vent session, but I feel that I would be doing you a disservice to write this book and leave this chapter out because I have learned something I feel the need to share. *True friends DO exist, but they typically are few and far between.*

I didn't come to this conclusion, though, until I decided to take a step back. I decided to just stop reaching out and just kind of stay in my own little world for a few weeks and spend time with my husband and babies because I didn't have much to give, and I wanted them to get anything I did have left to offer. In a sense, I purposely lived under a rock for a little while. This was actually recommended to me by my life coach. She suggested it one day after an emotional over-the-phone session when she said to me, "What is the worst thing that could happen if you just took a step back and focused on you and your family instead of putting so much pressure on yourself to check in on everyone else?"

I guess I had never really thought about it because I am naturally "that girl" that just routinely checks in on everyone. But I started really thinking about how good it would feel for someone to call me up and ask *me* how I was doing for a change. I was in a major funk, and I wasn't my usual happy and peppy self. I knew it was past time that I took the time to sort out my emotions and take time to focus on myself and work on healing. So, I decided to take her advice and just stop reaching out because I just didn't have it in me. I felt depression creeping back into my life, and I refused to go there again. So, I went into survival mode.

Do you know what then happened? A few friends did end up checking in on me. They reached out and asked me, "Hey, Laura, are you okay? I haven't heard from you in a while." They checked in on me and really wanted to know how I was really doing. They wanted my real answer, and they didn't put pressure on me to feel any other way than how I was really feeling. They didn't just want the "Things are good. Just staying busy with kiddos!" usual answer. They gave me a safe space to share my feelings and the hurt I had experienced. They prayed for me and came alongside me in my time of need, which inevitably helped me heal. Truthfully, it felt so good to not be the one reaching out, and it really made me feel loved.

Something else happened though. Some "friendships" that I had been putting so much effort into ended up dwindling away because they were as I thought. They were one-sided. Now, listen, I get that life is busy, but if a year has gone by and not once have they reached out to you, then I would say it's time to do some reevaluating of that relationship. Frankly, in this high-tech day and age, it takes five seconds to send a text to check on someone, so really, none of us have an excuse. Am I right, or am I right?

This all may seem like a silly and juvenile game that I played by stepping away and seeing who would reach out, but it was one of the best things I have ever done for myself emotionally. It's so easy to fall into an unhealthy, exhausting pattern in our relationships without us ever noticing. I think that, especially as moms, we get into the habit of giving so much of ourselves, yet in the meantime, our love cup and emotional needs go unmet. These unhealthy relationship patterns that sometimes we put into place ourselves can lead to major burnout. The fact is that even the most introverted person on the planet still needs to know that she is loved and that someone cares for her. *When we put too much pressure on ourselves to keep our relationships strong, we end up feeling depleted, and we don't give our true friends a chance to ever do their part and reach out. So, we are left feeling unloved and uncared for.*

If there is one thing that life has taught me, it is that true friendships are hard to come by, and they are pure GOLD. They will stand the test of time and hardships, and they will be there for you in the valleys of life. They will celebrate with you, laugh with you, cry with you, and meet you where you are. They don't one-up you, compete with you, or just join you in the highlight reel of life, but instead they join you behind the scenes. Now, though life may get crazy at times and weeks may pass, these true friends will always come back around, and you will be able to naturally pick up where you left off.

Please, don't drain yourself dry trying to keep up with surfacy relationships that aren't genuine, recip-rocated, or fulfilling. I can now count on one hand the close friends I have in my life, and I am so incredibly grateful for them. They are those ride-or-die, mutu-ally fulfilling relationships that I know aren't going anywhere. It may have taken me 'til thirty years old to be able to really recognize which friendships are gen-uine and worth my effort and time, but I would say it's better late than never, right? Now, who do you con-sider to be your closest of friends? Have they stood the test of time, hardships, and change? If so, hold them close, and thank God that they are in your life.

Speaking of thankfulness, today, as I write this chapter, it is ironically Thanksgiving Day. It is a gor-geous, sunny day, and I am just sitting here soaking up the aroma of the turkey roasting in the oven and the scent of my favorite cinnamon apple candle burning while the kids play outside with their dad. Sometimes I have to stop and just pinch myself because, man, I am so blessed. Though it's not been the easiest year with COVID changing all of our lives in so many ways, still, there are so just many things that I am grateful to God for. In fact, despite this year's hardships, it has actually been a year that I have grown the most. Now, if I were to write down everything that I am thankful for this year, it would take a really long time. If I were to narrow it down, though, and pick my top three things, I would have to say that, aside from my sweet family and my health, genuine friendships are for sure at the top of my list.

Communicating Your Needs to Those You Love

"*If* he would just take this baby from my hip so I could finish dinner." "*If* she would just let me go to the bathroom alone." "*If* she would just check in on me next week, it would mean a lot." "*If* he would just take the kids out of the house for an hour so I could get some things done." "*If* they would just stop leaving bits of kinetic sand all throughout the house." "*If* he would just offer to run this errand for me after work so I don't have to drag the kids into the store." "*If* he would just let me watch my favorite show on a Monday night instead of a stupid football game for a change."

If, if, if started a lot of my thoughts early in my motherhood career. I would often get so flustered that I remember sometimes inwardly just wanting to crawl under my bedcovers and cry.

Yet, I wanted so badly to play the part of a calm, cool, and collected mom that I often would keep what I needed or what drove me crazy to myself. I would get so frustrated that my husband would be sitting on the couch while I was making dinner with a baby on the hip, but I often wouldn't *tell* him that I needed help. A "good mom" can do it all, remember? I would often just want to cry when my chatty three-year-old little girl wouldn't let me even have a moment to pee alone, yet I still would let her come into the bathroom. What good mom locks their child out just for a moment of silence, right?

I would get so incredibly angry when I would clean up a room and then walk into another one and see it destroyed yet again. I always felt (and still do sometimes) as if I would go one step forward and then five steps back in the cleaning department when my kids would get to playing. Let me tell you, my kids are Tom and Jerry, through and through, and I know that chaos and messes are inevitable when raising young children. Yet, I wouldn't tell my husband that I needed him to take them out of the house to the backyard or on an errand for me to play catch up around the house. I remember one day actually wanting to cry when my kids asked me to get out the kinetic sand for them to play with because I knew what a mess it would make for me to clean up later. But guess what? I still kept buying it and letting them play with it!

Aren't kids supposed to be able to make a mess when having fun? Sure they are, but not at the constant expense of my sanity, they aren't! Sorry, not sorry. Listen, I can easily deal with a knocked-over toy bin, but Play-Doh or kinetic sand shoved into my carpet and dispersed all over the house? Yeah, no thanks, I'll pass. Now, these days when the kids are asking for either, I gently remind them, "Mommy can't handle the mess this makes in our home. Take it outside to the porch, kids, or we won't be playing with it at all." That is now my motto, and I have been much happier since I established it openly with my kids a couple of years back.

In a whole other scenario, I used to spend every Monday night during football season so irritated because I would spend them watching my husband yell at the TV every time another touchdown was made while I was missing my favorite shows. Yet I just sat there, irritated, and for the longest time, and I never told him. Side note: he now has a man cave with his own TV for a night he can't miss a game, and now I never miss my favorite shows anymore (*Dancing With The Stars* or *The Bachelor* are at the top of my list), so it's a win-win! But, it did take me one day communicating, "Umm, hey, babe? I actually really don't like watching football three evenings a week. Can we compromise and watch my shows on Monday night for a change? It would really mean a lot to me." It was a simple conversation about such a mundane thing, but nevertheless, it was something that needed discussion to keep me from building up resentment and just sitting there, frustrated.

For so long, I was such a people-pleaser that my frustrations would often build with my husband and kids over some of the most seemingly silly things. Yet, I wouldn't ever voice how I was feeling. Instead, I would just get downright resentful. I would walk around overwhelmed and frustrated; yet again, it was my lack of communication that was ultimately setting me off. I set myself up for frustration when I tried to play the part of a happy wife and mom who did it all with a smile.

We as women are givers and nurturers. It is often a struggle for us to voice our own needs and frustrations because many of us (and myself included at one point) have gotten into the habit of putting ourselves last. The thing is, though, we deserve a say too! We are human. We are allowed to get frustrated, annoyed, and stressed out. What is *not* okay, though, is for us to go about life never voicing it to those we love, expecting them to make sense of our emotions.

Be open with those you love. This includes your spouse, your kids, your family, and your friends. This inevitably will help keep you from building up resentment towards them, and it will allow you to catch your breath. Frustrations left festering on the inside will steal your joy. Love those in your life and yourself enough to be open and honest. You will thank yourself in the end, and they will love you for it in return.

Mom-Shamers and Joy-Stealers

Now, being a few years into motherhood, I honestly no longer doubt that I am a good mom, and I no longer need someone to tell me that I am in order to believe it. If I am being totally honest, though, I used to care way too much about what others thought about me, to the point of extreme anxiety. *The truth is I just never wanted to be labeled as "that mom."*

When I was pregnant with my daughter, I swore to myself that I would never be *that* mom with *that* kid having *that* meltdown. I never thought I was going to be that mom with the child still in diapers at age three. I never thought I would be that mom who raised her voice. I never thought I would be that mom who forgot to brush her kids' teeth or hair on occasion. I never thought I would be that mom who bribed her kids (we will touch more on this later). I never thought I would be that mom who would be late to school pick-up. I never thought I would be that mom with dirty laundry piled up to the ceiling or with a disaster of a house. And never in my wildest, health-nut dreams did I think I would be "that mom" whose child hated green vegetables with a passion and refused to eat the dinner I cooked and sometimes ended up eating a graham cracker with peanut butter instead.

But the truth is that sometimes I *am* "that mom," and you know what? I used to beat myself down about it, compare myself to others, and feel ashamed, but today I don't. People can stare and judge away. Their opinion of me is none of my business, so why do I care? Can I say that I am okay with everything I "fall short of" that I just mentioned? Not at all, and I absolutely think I always have room to improve. However, I know that I am doing my very best each and every day. God ingrained in me the truth a couple of years back that all He requires of me is my best. That's it. I don't have to keep up with everyone else.

I know some days will be harder than others. I know some days I won't feel that I checked all of my boxes and crossed all of my t's as a mom, but I know that God gave me my children for a purpose. *What I have decided is that I am okay being "that mom" because it means I get to be "their mom," and I am allowed to sometimes make mistakes.* "That mom" is the mom God created me to be. I am not required to be perfect, and neither are you.

Have you ever been made to feel, though, that you had to be? Have you ever had a playdate from hell where you were made to feel small and unqualified as a mom? Have you ever been "that mom" whose kid hits another kid to get him off the swing? Or have you ever been "that mom" who is digging at the bottom of her purse for a piece of gum to just keep your kid quiet in the waiting room? How about that mom who avoids restaurants with metal roofs in case, God forbid, their cell phone doesn't have access to their kid's favorite show or game? That's me. And if I have learned anything in my motherhood career, it is this: parenting is hard whichever way you slice it, and you and I don't have time for mom-shamers in our life. I'm sorry, but we just don't. *If your child or children are being fed, clothed, and loved, then you are doing a great job, and you need to protect yourself from anyone that makes you feel otherwise.*

Truthfully, I used to hesitate to take even a picture on date night and post it on social media. I used to think that someone would think, "Wow, they are on another date or another trip away from their kids?" But then I realized that I was downright proud to be spending time with my handsome husband and sharing and capturing our happy moments together. As we just discussed, our marriage has to come first in order for our children to thrive and feel happy and secure. So now I post away, and I don't think twice about it.

If we are all dressed up, you better believe we are going to document it. I don't rock heels very often, and when I do, I sure as heck am going to strike a pose. If I order a fun margarita, I am going to probably snap and share that too. If I get my nails or hair done and I am feeling extra pretty and pampered, I will probably take a selfie. I love time with babies so much, but I love time without them, too, and I document both parts of my life unashamedly. If something makes you happy, friend, you should feel free to share your joy! Excuse my slang, but *screw* your "image." Just be YOU.

Now, as I previously mentioned, I am not anti-screens, and I am not against bribing my kids to behave when we are out. In fact, I honestly think iPads and Yum Earth suckers (don't worry...they are organic and artificial-dye-free) are God's gift to every parent of young children. Now, hear me out. My kids get plenty of fresh air and playtime together, but they also have screen-time pretty much on a daily basis. My husband works two jobs, and sometimes this mama needs a break and a mess-free distraction for the kids, or sometimes the kids just need time to unwind. So, needless to say, we always try and make sure their iPads are fully charged.

So now I guess it's also time to admit that I bribe my kids with suckers. Wait, are you reading that right? Yes, you sure are. This may come as a big surprise to you if you know anything about me. I am a nutritionist, for goodness' sake! That being said, though I wish they did, my kids don't always behave in every waiting room or on every car ride. So yup, I bribe them with suckers once in a while when I am at my wit's end. Yes, you heard me right. We bribe our kids sometimes with a little sugar, and you know what? It works for us (*insert judgmental gasps*).

Now, bribing aside, sometimes we also reward our children for choosing to obey or when they practice self-control. For instance, we have rewarded our daughter for keeping her room clean for a week straight (something she struggles with) or our son for pooping in the potty instead of hiding to poop in his diaper. Now, it's not always a sucker. Sometimes it's a privilege of some sort or a trip to the dollar store (this especially works for my daughter in motivating her in school as well). Nevertheless, we sometimes reward our kids for their good behavior without shame.

Now, we don't reward every good behavior by any means. We, of course, want our children to grow up with a heart to obey and to do the right thing without getting anything in return, and so we discuss this with them often. We say, "When you practice obedience, it makes not only Mommy and Daddy happy, but it makes God happy!" So why, then, do we reward them on occasion? Shouldn't they just do what they are told with no questions asked? Yes, they should. But I also want to show them how much I appreciate their effort and teach them hard work pays off in the end. Bribing or having a reward system for your young children or whatever you want to call it may not be your parenting style, and that is okay, but don't knock it before you try it!

Sometimes, though, even with sucker bribes in the doctor's office and all, I am still "that mom" with her kid making a scene in public. I have been made to feel embarrassed at playdates. I have been stared down and gawked at. But you know what? Our kids are human, just like we are. They are not robots, and meltdowns and embarrassing moments are all part of parenting young children. There *will* be struggles and plenty of bumps in the road. We should all be in this together as mothers, should we not? We should be striving to bring each other up, shouldn't we? Yet, sometimes we get brought down by someone's hurtful, passive-aggressive comment or by someone's brag session over her seemingly perfect children that end up making us feel like garbage.

Maybe it's a mother or mother-in-law or an older woman who means well but has forgotten the struggles of the stage you are in. Maybe it is even a well-meaning friend or even your spouse. The fact of the matter is, though, that we are all trying our best, and as much as we all try not to, we already inwardly criticize ourselves enough. We don't need anyone adding to our mommy guilt.

Now, please don't misunderstand me. There are times where we need a good talking-to and/or we need some tough love. But in general, my motto is this: *"If I haven't asked you for your opinion on how to parent my child, then you aren't allowed to give it to me."* And to those who find the need to passive-aggressively tear you down in order to bring themselves up? I challenge you to clap back and ask them (out loud or inwardly), "Do you want a sticker because your child excels in an area mine doesn't or because you don't struggle the same way I struggle in my parenting? What is going on in your life that makes you feel the need to make others feel small?" Since I became a mom, I really do strive to tune out the negative, but sometimes they still get to me. I have one wild child and one calm child. I have one that wouldn't wean 'til well after he was two and a half. I have one that won't eat greens. I have one who loudly pronounces "chips" in the grocery store as "s***" loud and clear for everyone to hear.

Yes, I will say, though, that since I hit thirty, I really have made a conscious effort to not care what others think about my kids or me. How I parent is between me and God, and He sees and knows my heart and how hard I try. Also, if I am really self-reflecting, I have to ask myself if me stressing over my kids' behavior in public is actually about *them* or if it is about *me*. Is it about my image? Is it about others viewing me as a parent who has her crap together and who raises her kids "right"? Is my kid sitting still at a restaurant really important to me because I want him or her to learn to be patient and obedient, or is it about how others view me as a mother? The fact of the matter is God knows my heart, and He sees all of the effort I put towards raising my kids, and therefore *I don't have to prove myself to anyone, and neither do you.*

Now, please hear me out. It is okay; in fact, it is fantastic if your baby sleeps through the night at three months old; is potty trained at fifteen months; can write the entire alphabet by age two; eats everything you put in front of him or her; sits quietly through church or in a restaurant; wins a pageant; gets honor roll and then goes on to get a full scholarship to one of the most prestigious colleges in the country. But it is also okay if your children don't.

You don't have to "measure up" to anyone's standards, and neither do your children. All God asks out of us and our children is our very best in life. So, let's stop striving for perfect standards, and let's cut ourselves and our kids some slack! Lastly, let's remember that in this life, sometimes haters are just going to hate, and you know what? It's downright awful to have someone rip you down as a mother (trust me, I know). But if our confidence is in the Lord, does it really matter what others think about us? The answer is a resounding "no." It absolutely does not.

Learning to Say "No"

I get it. It's hard to say no, especially if you are anything like me, an avid people-pleaser. I want to help. I want to make everyone happy. I never want to let anyone down. But do you know what I have realized over the years? Oftentimes when I say "yes" to someone or something, I end up letting myself down in some way at the same time. It may be that I end up slacking on getting enough sleep, eating like I should, working out, or taking care of my home, which is ultimately supposed to be a place of peace and joy for my family and me. When I am overcommitted and I let my house or laundry go, my oasis quickly turns into a place of clutter, which in turn causes me stress. Then I get irritable at those around me and resentful towards my commitments because I feel like I'm drowning. It's a vicious cycle.

If I am being honest, most playdates and events that my husband and I host wear me out. It's not that I don't enjoy them because I really do! On the flip side, though, I am usually left with a large mess to clean up afterward, which usually takes up part of the next day. Does this mean that I say no to hosting anyone or anything in my home? No, it doesn't. But it does mean that I have learned to carefully decipher if it is the time for me to open my home or if it isn't. If I am already feeling stretched thin or overtaxed, it probably is not wise for me to add one more thing to my plate. The same goes for volunteering at church or school, and the same goes for those close to me. If I am feeling happy, at peace, and physically, mentally, and spiritually healthy, then sure, why not say yes? But time is precious, and I only have so much of it to give, so I have to really gauge my priorities, my current situation, and my health status before saying yes.

As a mom, it is easy to constantly feel touched out and needed, as we just discussed in the previous chapter. I once thought that this was just a feeling I had to accept, until one day I realized I had the power to say no to anyone, even my husband and my kids, at times. "Mommy, can we stay up a few minutes later?" "Mommy, can you get me this toy?" "Mommy, can we get out our paint sets?" "Mommy, can I go with you to the store?" "Hey, Laura, do you care if we host a New Year's Eve party at our house?" "Hey, Laura, can you stop by Home Depot for me after you pick us the kids from school?" "Hey, Laura, do you want to stay up late and finish watching the rest of *The Last Kingdom* series (it's on Netflix, and it's baller if you are looking for a new show)?" These are just a few random examples, but you get the picture. Sometimes I say "yes," but sometimes I say "no," and I try and do so *without guilt.*

"No, you can't stay up a few minutes later because it's time for Mommy and Daddy to clock out and take a break." "No, I am not buying that toy with one thousand tiny pieces for me to have to clean up and find it all over the house." "No, Mommy needs to go to the store alone to be as efficient as possible and to have a few minutes of silence to clear her head." "Sorry, babe, I just really don't think I have it in me right now to add hosting a bunch of people to the mix." "Sorry, babe, I really don't think I can swing into Home Depot right now. I have a client in a few minutes, and both kids are cranky in the back seat, asking to go home and have a snack." "Heck no, babe! I absolutely do not want to stay up late tonight. Today has been really draining, and I honestly just need to get some sleep. How about we just watch our show for an hour and then call it a night?"

Do you get what I am saying? Sometimes the healthiest and most loving thing we can do for ourselves is to say "no". We really have to weigh our yeses with our nos and not just jump to agreeing to something without thoroughly thinking it through. What or who are we saying yes to? Why are we saying yes? Will this hinder my health and happiness in any way? These are the questions we must ask ourselves before we say yes to someone or something. Does it mean that we never say yes to something that doesn't personally benefit us? Absolutely not. Many things God asks us to do require us to get out of our comfort zone and to sacrifice. But some things *are* optional. We can say yes, but we have to also be able to prioritize our health and properly manage our stress levels at the same time. Our oxygen mask has to go on first, remember? If we overextend ourselves, we *will* burn out and have nothing left to give to those we love, much less be able to enjoy life. So say "yes," but also practice equally saying "no." Again, it's an act of self-love and self-care.

Learning to Delegate

A mom with her sanity still intact typically has had to learn that there are times when she must ask for help. Sure, we want to do it all, but we just can't. We want to have a clean house, clean car, folded laundry, toned body, painted nails, and our sanity intact, but yet, we find that we can't seem to have all of our boxes checked. Can I let you in on a little secret? *You aren't supposed to have all of your boxes checked all at the same time.* If you can't handle a dirty house, piles of laundry, or you get cranky if you miss a workout, please know I get it because so do I. But that is why I choose to delegate.

For instance, I have been getting my house cleaned since I was pregnant with my second child. I was a burnt-out mama of a very energized two-year-old, and I needed to use her nap time to work, get ready for the new baby, or nap. I just ran out of time to clean. The only time that was left to clean was precious family time. One day I remember looking out my window and seeing my daughter being pushed on the swing by her grandmother. It was a sweet sight to see, but I remember sadly thinking, "That should be me." But yet I was stuck inside mopping the floor. So, one day I gave in and hired a cleaner to come every two weeks to my home, and I can't even begin to tell you how much more at ease and joyful it made me feel.

Another thing that was taking up my time and causing me stress was grocery shopping. I would spend two hours on a Friday, going down each aisle at Walmart and checking items off of my list. At the same time, though, I was also trying to entertain my wiggly toddler, who was *not* happy about being stuck in one place. It was such a drag, and honestly, I got to the point where I dreaded Fridays because I knew it meant I had to grocery shop with a cranky kid for two hours. Now that my kids are older, on the occasion when I do take them into a store with me, they ask me about one hundred and one times if they can have something, and they often will chuck random items into my cart that I often won't discover till we get home.

Listen, I love quality time with my kids, but shopping is just not something I enjoy with them. Shopping can be fun and therapeutic, but for me, I find it only is when I am shopping *alone.* Sure, I could suck it up and drag them into the store anyway, but why, when there are so many grocery delivery options available? As I have said before, I am all about the shortcuts and taking all of the help I can get so that I can keep my sanity intact. Now, if you love grocery shopping with your kiddos, then, by all means, have at it! But if it stresses you out like it does me, then why not take advantage of the services available in this day and age, right?

Truthfully, we are capable of delegating, but only *if* we let our pride go and admit we can't do everything, at least not without burning ourselves out. Also, I will remind you once again that we don't need to prove ourselves to anyone. I know my kids are capable of sitting still if I really want them to, but I still don't want to take them to the grocery store if I don't have to. As a busy mama, I try and keep it as easy on myself as possible, and I hope you will do the same. Though we may be able to "do it all," why stress ourselves out by trying? There is so much help available, especially these days! The thing is, though, we have to first be willing to admit we need help and then ask for it.

I want to encourage you to take an honest look at all you have to do and then be willing to delegate tasks where possible. I will remind you once again that you do not have to be Superwoman and do everything yourself. So, how about you let someone else help you for a change?

Letting Go of Resentment

Let's dive into resentment a little further because there really is a lot to this topic. For me, it all began in the early stages of motherhood. My daughter was my world. Yet, after many sleepless nights, weeks of sore, leaking boobs, and a husband who had to almost immediately go back to work during the day and then went to work building our dream home in the evenings, it hit me. I became resentful. I was left alone in our tiny one-bedroom apartment with our new baby girl, feeling lonely and anything like myself. Now, this may sound awful, and I agree with you that it does, but if I am being honest, I was so sleep-deprived that I even became resentful toward my innocent baby.

Call it hormones, postpartum depression, or just pure exhaustion, but I really did. Even though I knew she was just a baby and it wasn't her fault, I would inwardly resent the fact that she had caused me so much discomfort and fatigue. She wouldn't take a bottle no matter how hard I tried, so it was left up to me to physically feed her constantly. I also resented my husband for the freedom he still had. Though he was working extremely hard, I resented the fact that he could relatively live a "normal life" or one similar to the one he lived before our daughter was born.

Looking back, I recognize that at the time, I was unknowingly in the pits of postpartum depression but trying to hide it and just smile through it. I would bottle up how I felt, and I would just go through the robotic motions of caring for our daughter day after day. Yet if I am being honest, I had lost my spark and my joy. I was in total survival mode, and up until my daughter was four months old, I didn't leave her side once.

That was six years ago now. Fast-forward to having my son three years later. I had learned enough about myself to recognize when these feelings of resentment would start to creep up, and I would know that it was time to step away and give myself a break, ask for help, and do what I could to rest up. Yet even then, I remember being at a park a few months after he was born, when my toddler asked me to push her on the swing. At that time, my son was in a growth support and seemed to want to nurse every hour on the hour.

So there I was, stuck on a park bench, having to tell my little girl, "Sorry, baby, not right now. The baby has to eat." I felt guilty, and then I remember even feeling worse when I would see other moms who were out of the baby stage, pushing their older kids on the swing and giving their toddlers all of their attention.

What feeling do you think then crept up again? You guessed it...resentment. I was resentful and jealous of the women who didn't have bags under their eyes and a baby on their hip. I was resentful and jealous that they didn't have to push a bulky double stroller everywhere they went and that they had two free hands. Mostly, though, I was resentful because as much as I loved my baby boy, I was missing the time and freedom I had had with my daughter when it was just us, and I was upset and sad that it was taken from me.

Feelings of resentment are normal. They may not be healthy feelings to have, but I can tell you first-hand that, in motherhood, they can and do come up. Your life is different now. In many ways, your life has changed, and though you love your child or children fiercely, you often may miss the freedom you once had, and that is okay. What helped me eventually navigate through my negative emotions of resentment was to remember that life comes in waves. Some seasons are inevitably harder than others, and some of these harder seasons are the only way of passage to the next, less-challenging season.

Life is all about hills and valleys, and those hard seasons help us appreciate the more carefree, enjoyable ones. If you see a mother who looks like she has it all together, she very well might. But don't think for a second she hasn't put in her time in those hard stages too. Don't think for a second she hasn't spent her share of sessions crying in the shower. And don't think for a second she never felt as maybe you do now. If you are struggling and in a hard season in your parenting journey, know that it won't last forever, and one day it will all be a distant memory.

Now I miss those days when my babies were little, and I tell my husband all the time how I wish I could go back and relive them. Right now, as I am writing this chapter, I am sitting in an airplane with my husband, flying to Memphis, Tennessee. Our kids, who are now three and six, are back at home with family, and we are taking a little weekend trip away, just us. If you had told me three years ago, sitting on that park bench, nursing my infant son, that I would shortly have the freedom to travel again with my husband, sleep through the night, write a book, and take time back for myself, I would have rolled my eyes. It just seemed so far away, but really it happened in a blink of an eye.

So, know this: it's okay to not be okay or to be perfectly happy in the stage you're in. You're entitled to your emotions and your feelings. It's okay to daydream of regaining your freedom again. But don't lose sight of the fact that you will never be in this stage with this baby ever again. Time moves all too quickly. So, find joy in the little things. Soak up those baby giggles and kiss those chubby baby cheeks, and remember that this, too, shall pass.

Pursuing Your Passions and Following Your Dreams

What sparks your interest and brings you joy? What helps you break away and find freedom from the clutter of the world, and *what ignites your heart on fire?* These are the questions that we need to be asking ourselves often, especially in the midst of the first few years of motherhood, when it's easy to feel as though we've lost ourselves, and we often find ourselves struggling to rediscover who we are.

I know for me, in those early months of my daughter's infancy, I struggled with this. I felt as if all I did was nurse, burp, change diapers, clean the house, and do laundry. Needless to say, for quite a while, I can honestly say that I lost my "spark." I was in total robot mode, and though I can honestly say I was doing quite well in the mothering department, and my baby girl was well-cared-for and loved, I felt as if I was missing something. I was missing the old *me.*

Just to give you a little background on me, I have been writing since I was about six years old. My mom says that I would just sit down for hours and write stories while my other siblings were playing around me. Writing was my passion and still is. Three years prior to having my baby, I had started a blog at about the same time I began working as a nutritional consultant. I wrote, posted often about all things health and wellness that were of interest to me, and I shared my recipes as well. When I had my daughter, though,

I spent a good six months hardly writing at all or seeing clients, both of which I loved.

It all came down to the fact that I absolutely refused to leave my daughter with anyone in order to go back to work (even for a couple of hours), and I also didn't allow myself any time for writing and blogging because I was so determined to keep up with the house and laundry. When the baby napped during the day, I would do house chores instead of giving myself a break and a little time to do something I was passionate about. I was more worried about feeling and proving that I could "do it all."

Those few months I was not seeing clients were honestly really hard for me. I just loved and still absolutely love my role in helping others feel their best and naturally heal their bodies through nutrition. As special as those first few months were with my rainbow baby, they were also equally as hard as I so badly missed doing what I loved. I used to feel guilty admitting this, but now I know that there is no shame in admitting that the transition into motherhood for me wasn't all smooth-sailing, and that's okay.

Now, please don't misunderstand me. I am well aware that those months off were completely necessary for both the well-being of me and my baby (and I am a total advocate for paid maternity leave). However, it didn't change the fact that I was still missing doing something I loved and was extremely passionate about. I feel that God gave me the gift of encouragement and a passion for health and wellness for a reason, and I knew that I was meant to make a difference and help others. I struggled with transitioning from a full-time employee to that of a stay-at-home mom, and for a while I didn't believe there was any way I could ever do both, which both depressed and discouraged me. I felt like a fish out of water, to say the least, in juggling my new role as a mother.

Now, this last passion of mine may seem minuscule to some, but for years I also had enjoyed reading fiction each evening before bed to help me unwind and break away from the day. I had read hundreds of books over the last few years, prior to becoming a mother. The thing about me is that I am an overthinker and a bit of a worrier, and this bedtime habit helped give my brain the break it needed in order to better control my anxiety and get the quality sleep I needed. Then I would start each day with reading a devotional ("encouragement for today" devotionals off of www. crosswalk.com are my favorite!) that would get me started on the right note to proceed into the day ahead.

Unfortunately, when my baby girl was born, I also completely stopped reading and doing devotionals. In fact, I didn't crack a book again for the first time until my daughter was a few months old, when my sister forced me out the door to Starbucks for a much-needed mommy break. Let me tell you, reading those few pages with a cup of coffee was pure heaven! It truly wasn't intentional to ever stop reading or spending time with God, but by the time my head would hit that pillow each night, I was so exhausted that I could barely keep my eyes open, much less read! When I would wake up each morning, I had been up so often in the night, I felt as if I had never really gone to sleep. So, it just didn't happen. Looking back, I could have asked for help and allowed myself time to step away and to pursue and spend time doing the things I loved. I could have made more time for the Lord. But, life became a blur, and I just didn't.

Okay, so these are just my personal examples of what keeps my spark aflame and my heart happy. As you now know, aside from being a wife and mom, I love to read, write, spend time with God each day, and consult with my clients (and not necessarily in that order). But what about *you*? What do you love to do? Better yet, what do you feel you were made to do, and what brings you joy? Do you love to paint, sing, horseback ride, sew, hike, bake, or perhaps even work? What hobbies or activities excite you, relax you, and help you feel more like *you*? I challenge you to make a list of what those passions are and then take the time back for *you* to pursue those passions that you know you have been missing! When we strive to do this as mothers, we feel whole and revived and ready to give back more of ourselves to those we love. Pursue your passions once again, Mama, and rediscover who you are. It's never too late!

Staying Positive and Staying Inspired

I think it's safe to say that there is enough negativity going around in the world and on social media to sink a ship. That being said, I really believe that we get to choose, for the most part, what sucks up our mental energy and takes up our headspace. Most of the time, we get the choice to either surround ourselves with positivity or negativity. What we read, watch, and who we follow can uplift and inspire us or discourage us and bring down our spirit. So it is up to us to be extremely picky and choosy on who and what gets our attention.

Surrounding ourselves and filling our minds with scripture and positive affirmations daily is one way that we can keep our spirits uplifted and shun negativity, depression, and anxiety. Life as a whole can so easily weigh us down and leave us feeling defeated. Especially in motherhood, we need every bit of God-breathed scripture and positive quotes we can get, just to make it through some days. But if we stay in scripture and hold onto what God says is true, and we surround ourselves with positive affirmations daily, our entire outlook on life can transform. When we fill our hearts and minds with things above and words of encouragement, we will find that a cloud lifts, and we have more strength to take on each day.

Throughout the years, I have gathered and memorized several verses, quotes, and affirmations that I have found help keep my outlook positive and keep me focusing, working hard towards my goals and resting on Jesus instead of the trials of this world. On days where I feel weak or that I have lost my motivation, I have these reminders to encourage me and add a little pep back into my step! Allow me to share them with you! Put them on your bathroom mirror or in a place in your home that you tend to spend a lot of time in, and read them and recite them often.

My Favorite Inspirational Quotes

"She believed she could, so she did."
~ R.S. Gray

*"The things you are passionate about are
not random; they are your calling."*
~ Fabienne Fredrickson

*"Be happy for what you have, while
working for what you want."*
~ Helen Keller

*"There are so many great ideas in the
world, but the world is measured by great
executions."*
~ Whitney Headen

*"We cannot become what we want by
remaining what we are."*
~ Max Dupree

*"It is well to be up before daybreak, for
such habits contribute to health, wealth,
and wisdom."*
~ Aristotle

*"Breathe, darling. This is just a chapter,
not your whole story."*
~ S.C. Lourie

"If you get tired, learn to rest, not to quit."
~ Banksy

"Even the darkest night will end, and the sun will rise."
~ Les Misérables

"I'd rather learn to dance in the rain than worry if I have an umbrella for the rest of my life."
~ Nikki Rowe

My Favorite Bible Verses About Strength and Perseverance

"The Lord will guide you always."
Isaiah 58:11 NIV

"If God be for us, who can be against us?"
Romans 8:31 KJV

"The Lord himself goes before you and will be with you; he will never leave you nor forsake you."
Deuteronomy 3:8 NIV

"Cast all of your anxiety on Him because He cares for you."
1 Peter 5:7 NIV

"The Lord is with me; I will not be afraid. What can mere mortals do to me?"
Psalm 118:6 NIV

"The Lord stood at my side and gave me strength."
2 Timothy 4:17 NIV

"No one will be able to stand against you all the days of your life. As I was with Moses, so I will be with you; I will never leave you nor forsake you."
Joshua 1:5 NLV

"I can do all things through Christ who strengthens me."
Philippians 4:13 NKJV

"And let us not grow weary of doing good, for in due season we will reap, if we do not give up."
Galatians 6:9 NIV

"I have told you these things, so that in me you may have peace. In this world you will have trouble. But take heart! I have overcome the world."
John 16:33 NIV

"Whatever you do, work at it with all your heart as working for the Lord, not for man."
Colossians 3:23 NIV

Behind the Scenes

Words of affirmation are very important to me. If you have ever read or taken the quiz "the Five Love Languages," you may have an inkling as to which love language resonates with you the most. For me, aside from physical touch are words of affirmation. I love it when others encourage me, and I love to hear I am appreciated as well. "Good job, Laura!" "Great work today!" is what I so often longed to hear ever since I was a little girl.

Before I became a mom, the work I did was mostly out in the open. When I became a mom, though, and found myself mostly at home, I found that the work I did was mostly behind the scenes. I was busier and more exhausted than before I stayed home, yet I felt as if no one saw all I did, and that really got to me. Not necessarily because I needed to be praised for everything I did, but because I was a new mom who was totally out of her element, and I just really needed to be acknowledged and encouraged along the way. I struggled with feeling that what I did, though extremely significant in my eyes, just wasn't appreciated, and I wasn't getting the encouragement and shoutouts on the sidelines that I needed to keep on sprinting. This all goes back to me not communicating my needs as I should have, but more on that later in this chapter.

Again, I had a severe case of postpartum depression at the time, and I am sure my hormones played a big role in the feelings I was having, *but* nevertheless, they were my feelings. It's not that my husband wasn't kindhearted and encouraging to me. It's not that I didn't get checked up on by friends and family. But I just felt that I was running a marathon with no one in the stands cheering me on. From the late-night feedings, healing stitches, sore nipples, diaper changes, burping and swaddling, and so on, the newborn stage was one of the most physically intense and nonstop jobs I had ever had in my life. I felt as if I never clocked out, and I was running on fumes. *Yet behind the scenes, I felt unseen.*

Maybe I sound like I'm just pouting. "C'mon, Laura, women have done this for thousands of years. Why are you so special and needy?" Well, frankly, I wasn't then, and I'm not now. I'm just being transparent with you about how I felt in those early stages of motherhood (and sometimes still do) in hopes that if you are struggling with the same feelings, you won't feel so alone. The fact is that I was thrown into the cycle of motherhood and feeling like a fish out of water, and regardless of how many women had done this before me, it didn't change the fact that I felt as if I was running a never-ending race, and I missed feeling as if the work I did mattered to someone. Maybe it's that I made it look easy. Maybe it's that I tried so hard to never complain.

Regardless of the reason, I should have voiced that I needed more encouragement when I was in such a vulnerable state. I could have shared more with friends about how painful my recovery was. I could have shared more about how much I was struggling on so little sleep. I could have shared that I felt an incredible amount of guilt because I didn't feel bonded to my new baby. Yet, I didn't.

I remember half-jokingly thinking, "Don't I deserve a medal for all of this hard work?" In short, the answer was yes. Every mother on this earth deserves a medal because she's a BEAST, and parenting is hard, hard work. But unfortunately those medals don't really exist. In fact, I think the closest thing to it is a "push present" that the husband often buys for his wife as a "thank you for giving up your body for nearly a year to grow and give birth to our baby."

But there are no medals; there are generally no gifts (except for Mother's Day); and there generally isn't anyone clapping for you on the sidelines day in and day out from morning to night. You may have a supportive spouse, family, and friends, but the fact is, no one will ever see all you really do as a mom...and that's okay. It's okay because *God sees every single thing you do, every little bit of sleep you miss, every tear you cry, and every moment you selflessly give of yourself. He sees all that you do for your children, things that no one else may ever see. God sees you behind the scenes.*

So, if you are feeling unappreciated and unnoticed as I was, I want you to know that it's normal to have these feelings as a mom at times, and especially in the beginning. It's not wrong to want to feel appreciated and noticed for all you do. Even now, with the chaos of potty-training, sassy toddler meltdowns, early school mornings, the laborious task of strategically going through my kids' wardrobe to figure out what they have to wear and what they need (I had no idea how much planning would go into clothing children!), I sometimes still wish all I did wasn't so behind the scenes. I sometimes inwardly wish my husband saw more of what I do and how hard I work.

I mean, don't you just *love* when they come home to a messy house after work and after you have spent your day elbow-deep in diapers and laundry? I used to get so upset when he would come home and it looked as if I hadn't done anything all day when my baby was teething, had an ear infection, or was in a growth spurt. I could hardly put the baby down for enough time to brush my teeth, let alone clean the house! If I am being honest, we've had the argument a few times over the last six years that started with a "What did you do today while I was at work?" question that, let's just say, did NOT go well. Needless to say, now (and after some intense marriage counseling sessions), my husband knows what to say and what *not* to say to a tired mommy, and he now takes the hint when to help out!

So, these days what I try and remember is that we serve a God who sees us entirely (the Hebrew name for Him is "El Roi," aka, "the God who sees me"), and that in itself gives me fulfillment and peace. Our "reward" is found in all of our children's sweet smiles, their hugs, their laughter, and the security we are able to give them. Our "medal" is the badge we receive when we are blessed with the title of "Mommy" (a title some struggle for years to obtain and some never get to have).

So, Mama, your new role may not seem to get noticed by others as maybe your previous occupation did, but never doubt that God sees all you do behind the scenes and that you will be richly blessed for it in the end. One day when you get to Heaven, God will look at you and say, "Well done, my good and faithful servant." So, look forward to that glorious day.

Needing to be Needed

I want to be transparent with you and tell you that up until recently, I have been struggling emotionally in a very big way. I have been struggling because, though it was discussed and agreed upon, my husband had a vasectomy last year, and it recently really hit me that I will never ever be pregnant again or nurse another baby. We discussed it at length, and we weighed all the odds, with my mental health and high-risk status being at the top of the list. I had suffered from horrible postpartum depression and anxiety after both babies were born, and I also was considered high risk due to my miscarriage history and my gene mutation (MTHFR). Not to mention the cost of raising kids and the fact that we were finally getting more time for our marriage (the first few months after each baby were born weren't easy on our marriage), there were a lot of reasons we came up with that helped us both make the decision that we were done having kids. In every way, it just made sense. But, my heart wasn't ready to be done. In fact, I don't think it ever will be or would have been, no matter how many babies we could have gone on to have or how long we waited to close this chapter of our lives.

See, I was that little girl who carried baby dolls with her wherever she went. I was the teenage girl who babysat often and dreamed of one day having babies of her own to care for. And I was that young newlywed who caught that "baby bug" early on and was dying to get pregnant even though, financially at the time, we weren't ready. I am a nurturer. It's just in my blood. So to see my babies no longer babies and growing so fast before my eyes pulls on my heartstrings big-time.

Does this resonate with you too? Maybe you are in that waiting period as we were for a while, trying to decide how many children you were meant to have. Maybe you want another baby, but your spouse doesn't, or vice versa.

The reality is, most women feel called to be mothers, and most mourn seeing their babies grow up. Being a mom makes me feel validated. It makes me feel as if I am doing what I was put here on this planet to do, and it fulfills me in so many ways.

The truth is, I was that annoying girl you wanted to slap who, despite the high-risk pregnancies and the rocky road I went on to have my babies, LOVED being pregnant. I loved growing these precious babies inside of me, and I honestly felt great. I did have to inject myself daily with blood thinners, which wasn't fun, but I was just so grateful to finally be having a healthy pregnancy that I just didn't care. In fact, when my water broke with my son a few days early, I remember being a little sad because I wasn't going to be pregnant anymore.

I'm not saying my pregnancies were a total walk in the park for me, but I do think my perspective and gratefulness for being pregnant made it a very positive experience for me. Despite the struggles I've had, being pregnant was truly one of the best times in my life. So now, I've had to come to terms with the fact that those days are over, and somehow I have to be okay with it? No. How can I be?

The truth is, I actually *don't* have to be totally okay with it, and neither do you. I'm allowed to be sad and mourn that this stage is over. Yet, in many ways, at the same time, I can rejoice over how far I've come as a mom and be equally excited for the fun and awesome stages ahead! Also, we must remember that God will birth other things out of us once we are done having children. For instance, I have joked that my last book, *Live Healthy With Laura,* which I published last year, was my "third baby." It is something that took me months and months to create and produce.

In the same way, this book that you are reading (or my "fourth baby," as I am calling it) has cost me loads of time, emotion, and effort output as well. A couple of years ago, I would never have had this time to write as I do now. Now, don't get me wrong. I still have two small children, and it has still been quite a challenge, but nevertheless, God has given me more of an opportunity to write. I may not have a tiny baby to hold anymore, but God is giving me more time to use my gifts and grow.

You and I will always be needed by our children, no matter how old they get, but just maybe in a different way. They may not completely physically rely on us as much or at all anymore, but they will always need us to help support and guide them through this crazy thing called life. So, allow yourself to be sad today, but get excited for tomorrow and the many years to come that you will get to watch your children grow and discover the people that God meant for them to be. I can promise you that no matter how old your "babies" are, your job as their mother is never done, and you will always have a very special place in their hearts.

PART 3

Self-Care (The Spiritual)

"But the fruit of the Spirit is love, joy, peace, patience, kindness, goodness, faithfulness, gentleness, and self-control. Against such things there is no law."

Galatians 5:22–23

I love reflecting on the fruits of the Spirit. I believe that we as Christians should strive to be fruitful in each of these areas because they are a perfect reflection of the Spirit, which is a reflection of who God is. Ironically, I have found that these fruits of the Spirit, in many ways, each go back to the topic of self-care in one way or another. To love others and serve others, well, it begins with *us* caring for our temple in order to have the strength within us to be the hands and feet of Jesus.

Many say, "God will give you the strength to accomplish whatever He puts before you," and that is correct to an extent. But there will also be days that we feel as if we don't have it in us to do all we need to do, and therefore, as Christ carried His cross, we must rely on Him to carry us as well. But if we are to have the strength as mothers to press on and wake up each day at all, we have to do our part to care for the vessel He gave us *first*. We can't just expect our lack of self-care to not negatively impact our stamina and the drive needed for all of the tasks God has for us to do.

So now that we have broken down the aspects of our physical and mental health, let's talk about the spiritual. Let's dive a little deeper and examine each of these spiritual fruits and characteristics together that reflect who God is. Then let's see how each of these fruits can be linked back to our overall health.

Loving Well

"And now these three remain: faith, hope, and love. But the greatest of these is love."
                    1 Corinthians 13:13

I want to be known as a woman, a wife, a mother, a sister, a daughter, and a friend who loved well. I want those in my life to never doubt my love for them. I also want to be one who practices self-love and self-care and who speaks to herself in such a way as she would someone else that she loves. I believe that God wants us to reflect His love each and every day into the world through our dialogue and our actions. Oftentimes our actions and the way we present ourselves to others and the world are being watched without us ever even knowing. We are constantly being observed. Most importantly, our children are watching us minute by minute and observing how we treat others and how we treat *ourselves.* They watch how gentle and caring we are, and they see when we are less than gracious and caring as well.

Think back to the parables in the Bible. It's evident that Jesus took lots of time to be with those He loved. He found joy in caring and loving others. Yet, Jesus also knew His limits. He knew when He needed to take a break to be alone to pray and rest as He did several times in the Bible. He also encouraged His disciples to do the same quite often as well. Remember that time when He and His disciples were on a boat and the storm was raging and the winds were towering over the boat, yet He chose *then* of all times amidst the chaos to take a nap?

"And a great windstorm arose, and the waves were breaking into the boat, so that the boat was already filling. But he was in the stern, asleep on the cushion. And they woke him and said to him, "Teacher, do you not care that we are perishing?" And he awoke and rebuked the wind and said to the sea, "Peace! Be still!" And the wind ceased, and there was a great calm." (Mark 4:37–39)

Jesus took time to practice self-care, and *then* He woke up and calmed the waves. In a sense, He put on his oxygen mask first before helping others (remember at the time, he was a human as you and I are now). I find it intriguing that He didn't wait for everything to be going perfectly smoothly (pun intended) for Him to take the time to rest and care for His body. Though He was using this time as a way to test and strengthen His disciples' trust, I find it interesting in the way it all played out. Remember, though He was Jesus, He was born into this world a human, and therefore He had the same physical needs you and I have. *He knew that He needed to rest and practice self-love and self-care in order to have the strength to care for others.*

You know those crazy days where you feel as if you could pull your hair out and the kids are fighting; you're running late to everything; the house is a mess; and you burned dinner? Yeah, I have been there too. Do you think the answer in that instance is to keep pushing harder? Have you ever considered that it is *then,* most of all, that God wants us to take a breather and take time for a little self-love and self-care so that we don't bubble over and we have the strength to calm the storms in our lives, even if it means just fifteen minutes alone?

I believe Jesus knew that He had much to do and accomplish on this earth and that He had much love to spread, but yet He also knew His tasks required a lot of effort, and He knew better than to neglect His own physical needs. God has taught me in my own life that in order to love others well and in order to spread light in this world, I must follow His example, and I must make sure that my physical, emotional, and spiritual flame is first burning strong.

I can't help someone else or ignite their flame if mine is burnt out. Loving and caring well for my family, friends, and others require me to FIRST practice self-love and self-care (and no, it is NOT selfish). We should follow Christ's example because only *then* can we have the stamina to fully and wholeheartedly show others **love.**

Living Joyfully

> *"Consider it pure joy, my brothers and sisters, whenever you face trials of many kinds, because you know that the testing of your faith produces perseverance."*
>
> *James 1:2–3*

I once had a client who was a cancer survivor years ago tell me that the only way she had learned to get through the hardships of her life was to "CHOOSE joy" each and every day. Until then, I never really thought about joy as being a *choice*. Honestly, at that point in my life, I remember being in a place of sorrow and lacking a lot of joy that was once there before as I embarked on a path of infertility and depression. I remember also dwelling on the lack of money we had in our early married life and wallowing in self-pity. I remember letting the number on the scale depict how I felt about myself that day. (I was hanging onto a few pounds of "love chub" from our first year of marriage, and I wasn't happy about it.) I remember constantly being caught in the comparison trap of anyone my age who already had a baby, who already had graduated college, had a thigh gap, and had money to go on vacation. Years ago, I let my circumstances depict my happiness more often than not, and honestly, once in a while I still can catch myself falling into that trap.

In my early adulthood, I was impatient, and I was too focused on the seemingly negative aspects of my life and *my* timeline instead of God's timeline, instead of being focused on all of the blessings in my life (and there were a lot of them!). The ironic thing is that I have often been known as "the girl who sees life through rose-colored glasses." I am someone who many say reflects joy into the world, and I love that. But truthfully, there have been times when my life has gotten rocky, and I inwardly have let Satan steal joy from me and wreck my day. In my early twenties, I would spend days at a time in a negative spiral. When I decided, though, personally and prayerfully, to *choose joy* instead a few years back, everything shifted.

Trust me, I know that it is a lot easier said than done. But living joyfully is a fruit and characteristic that I strive for daily because I know it honors Christ. Not to mention, it makes life a heck of a lot more enjoyable when I am not so focused on all of its imperfections! The negative aspects of life will always be there, but what if we changed our perspective, counted our blessings a bit more, and made a conscious effort to choose joy instead of despair? This especially hits home to me since becoming a mother. Goodness knows there are days that are far from perfect and everything seems to be going wrong (#mamaneedsaglassofwine)! But our day is ultimately what we make it, right?

Here are some of the practical ways that I talk myself out of the "negativity trap" and choose JOY instead:

The negative attitude

"The house is a complete disaster! I would be embarrassed if someone walked in."

The joyful response

"I am blessed with healthy, mobile children who have the ability to run around and make messes as they happily play together. We will have a family cleanup session after dinner tonight, and I will just let them enjoy being kids for now."

The negative attitude

"I am swimming in laundry, and it just keeps piling up! I'm so overwhelmed!"

The joyful response

"I am blessed with a family that needs to be clothed. I will put the kids down for a nap, put on my favorite Netflix show or YouTube channel, set the timer for an hour, and then power through. It will feel so good to have it done! I've got this!"

The negative attitude

"I miss my postpartum body! My boobs sag, and I have loose skin on my belly."

The joyful response

"I was blessed to be able to grow a little human. Some people try for years and never can. I may have more curves now, but I am declaring my body daily as beautiful, sexy, and strong, and I am going to embrace my womanly, maternal body that brought life into this world...stretch marks and all! I have earned these stripes! I am beautiful and worthy of love and respect, and I will ONLY speak positively to myself as I would speak to my daughter or a friend."

The negative attitude

"Money is tight, and I wish we could do more outings and vacations as a family and make birthdays and holidays more special."

The joyful response

"If we are together as a family, then we are making memories together, no matter where we are! We don't need an expensive vacation or lavish holiday or birthday party to make life sweet. As long as my family feels loved and we are all together, then we are rich in the most prominent of ways and in a way money cannot buy!"

Do you see what I mean? Joy really is OUR choice! Even in the pits of my depression years ago, I remember that I would make myself sit down and write ten things each day that I was thankful for. Guess what? Even on the darkest of days, this little writing exercise shifted my whole perspective! As mothers, we feel this responsibility to our children to give them the world, and it is very easy to get down on ourselves and feel that we are not being enough or doing enough for them. But maybe what our culture has made us believe equals "the world" is actually garbage. Have you ever thought about that?

Can we talk about finances for a minute? I think we can all agree that money can be a huge stressor on a marriage and family, and it's one of the first things to get us down and steal our joy. My husband and I may be steady and stable now, but I remember the days when we were first married when we had a whopping $35 left after bills to go to the grocery store (yup, true story)! Now, thirteen years into our marriage, we are financially in a different place, with steady jobs and income, but it took a lot of dedication, hard work, and time to get here. Some people may look at you or me, who now have hit a point of financial stability in our lives, and think that it was just handed to us. But we know that it wasn't.

If you are at a low point in your finances or are at a starting point in your marriage or career, I am urging you to not get discouraged, and please stop comparing yourself to others who are at a different place in their lives. Most people you see who you deem as "successful" or who have "got it made" started from the bottom of the barrel and had to work hard to get where they are today. You will reach that point too! Just keep swimming!

Anyway, moving on, the point I am trying to make is that if you have been caught in the trap of thinking that the amount of money you have to your name is tied to the level of joy and satisfaction in your life, then first off, stop scrolling through that social media highlight reel (you aren't seeing the whole picture), and second off, ask God to change your perspective. You are giving money too much power in your life and over you, my friend. You can't take it with you when you leave this earth, and it doesn't belong to us anyway, right? So why hold it in such high regard? If you ask God to change your outlook on your finances and give you more of a grateful heart in your everyday life, then I promise you He will! He did for me. When you do this, I can promise you that your joy will increase exponentially!

Who cares if you can't afford designer clothes for your kids or you get their toys from the dollar store? Your kids sure don't know the difference, and none of that really matters! It *only* matters if we let it matter and if we teach our kids that it does. What I have found to be true is that joyfulness is often picked up from a young age. It starts from a child observing his or her parents and seeing how they carry themselves day to day and through the ups and downs of life. If we want our children to have this joy, it is up to *us* to be an example to them. Something as simple as saying on a beautiful day, "Wow, God really took out His paintbrush, didn't He?" can change children's whole perspective and allow them to look at their day and their life in a more positive light.

My grandmother used to say this all of the time when I was growing up, and it has become one of my favorite sayings to say to my kids. I never want them to just let a pretty day pass on by without stopping to acknowledge the beauty in it! When we teach our kids to have a positive and grateful outlook on life, they will carry that outlook into adulthood. I know this firsthand from experience to be true. Allow me for a minute to give you a glimpse into my childhood.

I was born in Winston Salem, NC. I am the second oldest of six kids. My dad was in residency at UVA medical school when I was born, and we lived in a tiny little house. When I was eighteen days old, a tornado came and destroyed our home. It was tragic. My mom still tells the story of how she had to hide my older sister and me under our dining room table as a tree fell on our roof. Needless to say, we had to start all over. My dad had to continue with his residency, so my parents had to be apart for six months as my mom went and stayed with my grandparents, with a newborn and toddler, and attempted to house hunt at the same time.

Flash-forward 'til I was a few months old, when we finally found our little nest in Fredericksburg, VA, where my dad was able to secure a job, and we all were able to be together again. We still had no money. In fact, on my very first Christmas, my parents couldn't afford Christmas gifts, so my mom made a doll for both my sister and me. It may not have cost a thing, but we didn't know the difference. We may have been a very low-income family at the time, but my parents were so happy to finally be reunited, and my sister and I were loved and we were happy.

A few years down the road and four more kids later, we were a Brady Bunch–sized family. We were homeschooled and each other's playmates. Though financially we were better off at that point, my family still had hardships, but my parents never made our hardships the center of our existence. My parents always taught us to pray and thank God daily at the dinner table and before bed for what He had given us and what we were thankful for that day. As children, we felt happy and loved, and we made most of our memories in the backyard together, playing house, climbing trees, or exploring the nearby creek in ways that didn't cost a dime. Life was good, and we were taught to appreciate "the little things."

Today we are all still tight-knit as siblings, and I think I can speak for all of us and say that we still carry that positive and grateful outlook that was taught to us from a young age, and we are all very grateful for it. When I find myself slipping back into a negative way of thinking, I think back to my childhood, and I am reminded that real joy doesn't cost a thing. Then my negative emotions and thoughts quickly start to disappear the second I get out my pen and notepad, and I start counting my blessings!

The point of me telling you all of this is so that you will put less pressure on yourself in general, but *especially* as a mother. *This ultimately is one of the best ways we can practice self-care and self-love and keep our stress levels in a healthy state.* Stop putting pressure on yourself to "give your child the world." What does that really mean anyway, and who's to say what children "must have" to be happy? I think half of the reason we often find ourselves depressed and in a negative spin of emotions is because of the extreme expectations we and our culture both put on us.

Let me let you in on a little secret. Your kids really don't care about "having it all" in the world's terms. They just want you to love them, get to know them, and spend time with them. If those three boxes are checked, then *choose joy,* Mama, because you are making a huge and lasting impact in your little ones' lives! By showing our children that we *choose joy* daily, I believe they will grow up as well to do the same, and they will have a good grasp of what really matters most in this life and dwell less on the things of this world.

Living in Peace

"Peace I leave with you; my peace I give you. I do not give to you as the world gives. Do not let your hearts be troubled and do not be afraid."
John 14:27

Life can shake us and leave us feeling helpless, anxious, and in pain. Oftentimes we don't know where to turn. Sometimes we get so overwhelmed with the everyday physical and emotional demands that we struggle to get out of bed in the morning. I know for me, starting out in my motherhood journey, I was constantly anxious. I was anxious about my baby girl's well-being, if she was breathing, eating enough, and pooping enough. Then I would be worried about how I was going to handle her when she started crawling and walking in our tiny one-bedroom apartment that was impossible to fully babyproof. Then I would worry about how I would handle her when she was older, what type of child and teenager she would be, and so on.

I would also worry about us financially. I was at that time only working half the amount of hours I had worked in years, and though my husband had a new job, we were building a new house, and we had new expenses coming up seemingly every second. The truth is, I lacked a lot of peace in my heart and in my life at the beginning of my motherhood career because I spent more time worrying about all of the "what-ifs?" and less time praying and asking God for peace and direction. God had brought us so far, but yet in this new stage, I felt shaken by the sudden changes and turns my life had taken, and I mistakenly thought I had to have it all figured out.

In reality, though, I didn't have to have anything figured out. I just had to keep going and believing that God would guide me in my parenting, in my relationship with my husband, in our finances, and in the midst of all of the "what-ifs." I had to learn to really trust Him like I never had before. In the midst of the unknowns, I had to believe and never doubt that He was always working in a miraculous way behind the scenes, even when I didn't see it. When I felt that we were lacking resources, I had to trust that He would provide as He always had.

Aside from my internal struggle with peace, I had to address my environment. Psychiatrists believe that physical clutter in our surroundings contributes to mental clutter and stress, which is the perfect recipe for a lack of peace. Back then, as much as I considered myself to be a neat freak, I was also equally a hoarder. We lived in a tiny apartment, yet I just couldn't bring myself to let things go. Even clothes that I had not worn in years were still in my not-so-roomy closet. Then, add a new baby on top of it, with all of the furniture and gadgets that brings, and you can imagine that I felt quite swamped.

Honestly, my tiny house was an organized disaster, and it really started driving me crazy. When I would walk through the door, I instantly felt overwhelmed and unsettled. I had accumulated too much stuff, and it had nowhere to go. So one day I decided something had to change, and so I grabbed a trash bag and I got rid of whatever I had not worn or used in a year. I cannot even begin to tell you how much it helped me rediscover peace in my home! So needless to say, these days "less is more" is the new motto in our house, and I intend to keep it that way!

Learning to be Patient and Wait On God

"I waited patiently for the Lord; he inclined to me and heard my cry."

Psalm 40:1

This one's a hard one, especially for me. I think back seven or eight years ago, when I was in the thick of infertility. I would find myself pregnant, only to lose the baby a couple months later. This happened several times in a row over a period of two years, and it was heart-wrenching. I remember thinking, "God, I know you put it in my heart to be a mother. Why are you allowing me to go through with this? We have finished school, and we are on our feet financially. *Now* is the perfect time to have a baby! Please, God, let me carry a pregnancy to term."

This was my prayer that I would pray over and over again, but the months would pass, and still, I felt as if God wasn't hearing me. It was honestly one of the hardest, loneliest periods of my life. Not lonely in the sense that I didn't have my husband, family, and friends to support me, but in the sense that my heart longed for a child to love, and nothing and no one in the world could fill that void. It also wasn't easy that several of my closest friends and a couple of family members were pregnant. I remember how, every couple of weeks, I would receive another baby shower invite in the mail, and again I would ask God, "When will it be my turn?"

I was wallowing in despair until one day, it hit me. God's silence wasn't Him shutting me out or saying no, but instead, God was telling me "not yet." Fast-forward two years, a blood-clotting disorder diagnosis, and over three hundred Lovenox shots later, and I was finally a mommy! It wasn't in my timing but in God's, and looking back, I see why He wanted me to be patient and just wait on Him. If we had gotten pregnant when we had actively started trying, my husband would not have had his current job. Little did we know at the time that it would take months and months for him to find a job as a physicist after graduating college. By the time we had our baby girl, he was working an amazing job with benefits, and we were able to afford for me to stay home. If our daughter had been born any earlier, it would not have even been an option. I would have had no choice but to go back to work.

Oh, do you want to hear another crazy curveball that we were thrown? You know those Lovenox injections I was just talking about? Yeah, my insurance at the time didn't want to cover them, and they were going to cost around a whopping five hundred bucks a month! Let me just remind you that when I found out I was pregnant, my husband was still looking for a job, so paying that sort of money out of pocket wasn't possible for us at that time, but clearly we had to find a way. So my dad (who is a family physician and also my boss) called around to other local offices, trying to see if anyone had any they could donate. After a few calls, he was able to find an office willing to donate a few months' supply to me, which was an amazing answer to prayer!

But the emotional backstory is that an elderly man's wife, who was one of their patients, had just passed away. Before she died, she needed these injections every single day to stay alive. When she was gone, her husband knew she would want them donated so that way they could bless someone else. Well, that someone else was me, or should I say...my baby girl. The woman's passing, in a sense, brought my daughter life. She passed away about the exact same time I conceived my daughter, and it gives me chills just thinking about how God works and His timing. I like to think that that man's wife, whoever she was, was smiling down from heaven when she saw my baby girl enter this world. Call me sentimental, but to this day, I could just cry just thinking about it.

So, if you are feeling as if you are just wading back and forth in life and thinking that God is not hearing your prayers, just know that He is always working behind the scenes, and His timing is always perfect. He may not always answer us how or when we want Him to, but just trust that He truly has your best interest in mind. When you think his silence means "no," God very well may just be saying "not yet," and one day you will be able to look back, connect the dots, and thank God that your prayers were not answered in your timing but in His.

Bestowing Kindness

"Kind words are like honey, sweet to the soul."
Proverbs 16:24

What does it mean to be kind and to show kindness to one another? Well, by definition, kindness is defined by three words: friendliness, generosity, and consideration.

kind·ness
/ˈkīn(d)nəs/

noun
the quality of being friendly, generous, and considerate.

Kindness is about thinking of one's needs and meeting those needs without a person having to ask. It's about being available as a listening ear, and it's about reflecting Christ's love on others, even if it is not reciprocated. It is about speaking to each other in love, and not in bitterness or anger. It's about being a light in this dark world.

But in order to be able to show kindness to others, we have to first practice being kind to *ourselves.* For us to reflect anything onto others and into this world, it must first come from within. Now, it's no secret that we are our worst critics, and we are constantly analyzing everything down to our appearance, our feelings, our thoughts, and nearly everything we do. We put ourselves under a microscope, and oftentimes we tear down ourselves and speak to ourselves in a way that we never would anyone else.

Why do we do this? Why do we not practice showing the same kindness that we show to others to ourselves? If we believe others around us deserve kindness, then why don't we?

"I am so stupid! How could I have missed that turn?"

"What is wrong with me? Can I ever make it anywhere on time?"

"Ugh! Just look at my thighs in these pants."

"Whoa, my hair is looking like a hot mess today."

"I never say the right things. I'm so awkward in social situations."

"I can't believe I forgot to pack her a snack for school. Mom of the year award right here!"

Now, I know I'm not the only one who has treated or spoken to herself this way at one point or treated herself with less kindness than she should have. But as acceptable and routine as it may seem to tear ourselves down on the daily, it still doesn't make it okay. First ask yourself if you would speak to anyone else in this way. Maybe think of your best friend, your mom, your husband or your child or even a stranger. If you wouldn't speak to them this way, then what the heck are you doing speaking to yourself that way? This may seem like I am beating a dead horse and going back to the topic of "love," but kindness is a little bit different than that. I think kindness has a lot to do with our actions, but it especially has to do with dialogue, starting with ourselves.

Are you being friendly, considerate, and generous in the way you are caring and speaking to yourself? If you have found yourself lately being less than kind to yourself or in any way, then let me start by reminding you that you are beautiful inside and out and *worthy* of kindness from others, but most especially from yourself. Did you ever hear the saying, "If you don't have anything nice to say, then don't say anything at all?" This applies to the way we speak to others and to ourselves.

Also, let's not forget that if we have children, they are constantly watching and observing what we do and say. I don't want my daughter to hear me talk down to myself about the cellulite I have on my thighs or hear me call myself an idiot for forgetting to buy eggs at the store. I want my children to hear me speak to myself and to others in a loving, kind manner that reflects Christ. I also want my children to be able to recognize when someone is not speaking to them kindly and know when to walk away. But how will they be able to recognize this if they hear it within their home and from their own parents?

It says in the Bible in Ephesians 2:10. "For we are God's masterpiece, created in Christ Jesus to do good works, which God prepared in advance for us to do." Do you know what that means? You and I are God's beautiful creation that He made for a *purpose*. We were not created by chance or by mistake, and therefore we are to be treated with respect, love, and kindness. Remember what kindness by definition means? Kindness means "the quality of being friendly, generous, and considerate." Ask yourself, are you being friendly to yourself and to others, generous in caring for your needs and the needs of others, and considerate of your feelings and the feelings of those around you?

If kindness towards others and to yourself is something that you need to work on, then well, join the club. This one isn't easy at times! But if our goal is to reflect Jesus, then kindness has to be something we commit to working on daily. Start today with first building yourself up in some way. Even something as simple as an affirmation, such as "God has made me confident; God has made me beautiful; and God has given me the strength I need to accomplish today's tasks," makes a huge difference. In fact, I still hold onto the affirmation I wrote while pregnant, when I was struggling to find peace with the number on the scale. I had been struggling with negative body image for years, and so each morning and each time I would get on the scale, I would say out loud, "I am happy. I am happy, and I am growing a beautiful baby." Really, it changed my whole perspective!

I challenge you to write an affirmation of your own on a Post-It note and put it on your mirror for you to see and say out loud each morning. You will be amazed at what a positive spin it puts on your entire day!

Reflecting Christ's Goodness out into the World

"Therefore, as we have opportunity, let us do good to all people..."

Galatians 6:10

God calls us to live in this world but not be of it. What this basically means is that we are called to stand out as Christians and be a light everywhere we go. When Christ walked the earth, He always strived to do good deeds and care for others each and every day. He used his human body or vessel to do acts of good to encourage and bless others everywhere He went. I want to do and be the same and walk the walk that Jesus walked while He was here on earth. I want to be a light!

If you really stop to look around, it is easy to find someone who looks worn down and in need of a smile, a few encouraging words, or a hug. But so often we get so caught up in our own lives that we forget to stop and actually look into the faces of others. How often do we drop our kids off at school or run into a store without even looking up to see who else is around us? We run in and run out as fast as we can so that we can move on to the next thing on our to-do list. We get stuck on the hamster wheel of life, and we forget to acknowledge others that come into our paths along the way.

It's so easy to do, and if I am being honest, sometimes I like to stay in my little bubble. I am an ambivert, so I require both people time and alone time, and if I haven't had enough alone time in a while, well then, honestly, the *last* thing I want to do is have a conversation with another mom at school or the cashier. But how many hard days have you had where a smile or an encouraging word from someone could have turned your whole day around?

When I was in the thick of my postpartum depression, I felt more alone than ever. I found myself going from working a full-time job, with coworkers I loved dearly, to being alone at home with my new baby girl. It was truly such a blessing to have the opportunity to be home with her, but yet still, I felt so alone. One thing I would do just to get out of the house in the first few weeks (before getting suddenly called back into work) is go for walks and push Scarlett in the stroller around a nearby neighborhood. After a couple of months of walking there, I came across an older woman who lived in the subdivision named Leslie, who would walk her dog, Libby, about the same time I would go on my walk each day.

This sweet lady always took a moment to say hello and smile at Scarlett and me and ask how we were doing. Over time I started looking forward to seeing her even though I really didn't know her very well. It was just really felt nice to see another familiar smile. I was missing my coworkers, and I felt isolated at home, trying to adapt to my new life as a stay-at-home mom. Yet, as I have already shared with you, I hid my depression and anxiety well. No one, not even my husband, knew how I was suffering at the time.

Anyway, as time went on, my conversations with Leslie went on a little longer and got a little deeper, and I eventually discovered that she was feeling just as lonely as I was. She didn't have a husband or children, and her extended family lived out of town. She worked from home, and she felt just as isolated as I did in my new role. It was around Thanksgiving one year where she confided in me how hard the holidays were for her and how she had been suffering from depression herself. Honestly, I would have never guessed that she was struggling in this way because she always seemed to have a smile on her face (but wait, so did I).

It was then, on that cool day in November, that I realized how important it was for me to snap out of my own little world from time to time and take time to acknowledge others. *God wants to use us to bless others in need, but He can't if we never look up.*

The truth is, everyone is going through something and in need of some more encouragement in their lives. So many people are suffering from depression and loneliness and are in need of a smile or a few kind words. Yet, they often feel overlooked. I don't know about you, but I never want to ever get so busy and wrapped up in myself that I pass by someone who is hurting and feeling alone and miss an opportunity to bless them with at least a smile. Leslie taught me the importance of this when I was in need of encouragement and companionship the most. She took the time to smile and say hello to me each and every time I walked by, even though she herself was suffering and feeling alone on the inside.

God wants both you and me to bless someone today. Remember, we don't come into contact with a stranger or another individual by mistake. God directs our paths and puts people on them for a reason. It is up to us to look up and look around while we are on these paths. Sometimes it may mean that we are pushed out of our comfort zone or that we are inconvenienced, and that is okay. God promises that when we take the time to bless others, we will be blessed and filled with joy in return. In fact, I found that one of the best anti-depressants there is, is to look to the needs of others. When we take the time to bless someone, even in the simplest of ways, God lifts our spirit and gives us such an incredible feeling of fulfillment and joy.

No matter how deep the pit of depression, anxiety, or despair that you are in, I want you to know that God wants to use you, and He is counting on you to bless someone else today. Yes, even at our lowest point, God can and will use us to better His kingdom. As worn down as you may feel, someone nearby needs to see your smile and hear your kind words. Someone today is in need of *you* as much as you may be in need of *them.* So, let's look up as we go about our day and share His goodness and light with those that come our way. Whether it be a smile, a hug, a meal, or a word of encouragement, let's strive to be a light in this dark, often-despairing world, and let's you and I and bless someone today.

When you look beyond yourself and strive to love others better, you may just find, as I did, that the cloud of depression and loneliness that haunts you is lifted, and your joy is once again returned to you, at least for a little while. Truly, one of the best anti-depressants on earth I have ever discovered is loving and looking to the needs of others. When we do this, our stress instantly diminishes, and we are filled with His joy and peace. This is not to go against what I have preached all throughout this book, that we first must put on our oxygen masks before attempting to care for others. But it *is* to say that once that is done, we are to be on the lookout for someone in need and try our best to love others as Christ did.

Living Faithfully

> *"Well done, good and faithful servant. You have*
> *been faithful over a little; I will set you over much.*
> *Enter into the joy of your master,"*
>
> *Matthew 25:21*

"Nope, not today, Satan!" Gosh, I can't even tell you how many times I have declared these words. How often do we wake up, excited to greet the day, only to find ourselves discouraged and ready to give up by the time lunchtime rolls around? How many times in life do we look up into the sky and ask, "Really, God?" The truth is, life is downright hard sometimes, and being a Christian and a believer doesn't necessarily mean an easier life. When life feels hopeless and we feel bled dry, it is easy to lose sight of God and His promises. It is easy to lose faith. But nevertheless, and no matter how hard life may get, God still remains faithful to us, and He always has our best interest in mind. He only asks us to trust Him and be faithful to Him in return.

God doesn't say in the Bible that, as humans, we aren't allowed to get discouraged, and He doesn't tell us that a life devoted to Him will always be smooth-sailing. But God *does* ask us to trust Him and be faithful regardless. He also promises us that we will be blessed for our faithfulness and commitment to Him in return. God promises never to abandon us, and therefore He asks the same devotion from us as well.

"Faithfulness" in the Bible means something quite different than "faith." Faith in God means trusting Him and relying on Him alone for our salvation. "Faithfulness" is referring to *devotion* and *commitment.* The fruits of the spirit remind us that in order to be fruitful, we must be committed to God and His plan for our life, even if at times we aren't sure what that is. Faithfulness means that when things get rocky, we look to Him to guide us, and we remain steadfast in His plan for our life. We don't jump in and out of a relationship with Him, depending on our circumstances. We prayerfully go about our lives and ask Him to guide us and show us the way.

How, though, is God supposed to speak to us and guide us if we never take the time to pray and read His word? *How else are we to hear His voice?* We must put God first and keep Him as our highest priority. However, as human beings with selfish hearts and a sinful nature, sometimes this is easier for us to say than do. If I am being honest, most days, I struggle to get my daily devotional in. Some days my time with God goes smoothly, and others, well, not so much. Most days I wake up early enough to be alone with God, but then sometimes my three-year-old will wake up five minutes later, requesting a snack and cartoons. Or I will be in the middle of going through my prayer list that I keep on my phone, but then my phone will ring or an email will pop up that I will be tempted to respond to.

Yes, Satan does everything he can to make my "quiet time" as chaotic as possible, but I do my best to not give in. I try my best to ignore that call or email and to quickly give my son a snack and get right back to my quiet time with God. But again, this is easier said than done. It requires serious commitment, and it requires us to be *faithful*.

Satan wants nothing more than to distract us and tempt us to break our commitments we have to God and to take our focus off of what God has for us to do. Satan wants to occupy our thoughts with anything and everything other than God. He wants to keep us so busy and distracted that our time with God falls to the wayside. But we must stand strong and resist him. He wants nothing more than to keep us away from God and the hope he offers us and keep us in a pit of despair. But we can't let the enemy win!

God promises that when we are faithful and loyal to Him and we work each day to have a relationship with Him and to glorify Him, we will be blessed in return. It sure as heck isn't always easy, but remember that Satan only has power over us *if* we give it to him. God is on our side, and He is stronger than the enemy. It says in 2 Thessalonians 3:3 that "the Lord is faithful, and he will strengthen you and protect you from the evil one." So, in the same way that we make vows to our spouse on our wedding day to be faithful, we are to make the same vow to God. When we are devoted and faithful to God, we can trust that He, in return, will give us the strength we need to face each day. When we stay close to God, then the enemy will flee!

Now, how does this tie into health and self-care? Well, when we are faithful to God, He promises all throughout the Bible that He will bless us and protect us in return. Among His blessings and protection come His supernatural strength. With His supernatural strength also comes the discipline we need to faithfully care for ourselves each day so that we have the stamina we need to do His work and to rock each day. All we have to do is ask Him for it. God tells us in John 16:24, "Ask and you will receive, and your joy will be complete." The kicker is, though, that *we* have to be willing to do the work and take the correct steps daily toward caring for our health. We must be faithful and committed to our well-being so that we may be strong for the hills and valleys ahead.

Listen up, Mama. No matter how hard life may get, stand strong, and remember that when we are faithful to God and are devoted to caring for our temple, Satan canNOT win. Stay faithful to the One who created you; ask Him to strengthen you and guide you daily; and He *will* protect you and give you His strength. This is His promise to us!

Learning the Art of Gentleness

> *"Be completely humble and gentle; be patient, bearing with one another in love."*
>
> *Ephesians 4:2*

God is a gentle God, full of love, compassion, and grace for us. He doesn't come at us with anger, harsh words, and ridicule. In the same way that God is gentle with us, are we called to be gentle with others, including ourselves. We aren't to come at others confrontationally with blazing guns. We aren't to rip each other down in an effort to make a point or prove that we are right. No, God calls us to be gentle.

God is a safe place for us, and therefore we are to be a safe place for others, especially our children. Our children aren't supposed to be afraid of us or terrified to tell us they messed up. They should know that we love them and that that will never change, no matter what mistakes they may make. They should know that when they come to us with their heads down, we will cover them with grace and love and not lash out at them in anger. With us, our children should feel secure.

In the same way that we are to be gentle to those we love and know, we are also to be gentle with those we don't personally know. This includes social media, mommy forums, and so on. Bear with me for one moment while I vent, will you? One thing I absolutely cannot stand is when I see mothers tearing down other mothers on the internet. I myself am a member of a few mommy forums on Facebook, and typically they are wonderful platforms that offer community, advice, and support. But then sometimes these platforms become a place that mothers use to bash and scrutinize other moms for things such as vaccinating their children, feeding their baby formula, or giving their child with an ear infection antibiotics.

Listen, it is one thing to lovingly state your opinion on a topic, and then it is another to rip someone down for theirs. I will say it again. As long as you are doing your best to care for and love your child in the way God leads you, then that is all that matters! You and I don't have to see eye to eye on everything or parent the same way to be in community with one another. Mothers should build each other up and speak to one another with gentleness, compassion, and love, whether in person or behind a screen. If someone is being harsh toward us, we are given the choice to not respond and to walk away. We are given the choice to rise above the scrutiny and move on. By doing this, we are reflecting Christ and treating others how He wants us to treat them.

Lastly, in the same way that God wants us to be gentle with others, He also wants us to be gentle with ourselves. This means that we give ourselves grace and room to be imperfect and to make mistakes. It means that we speak to ourselves in love, and it means that we don't ridicule ourselves for our every fault. It means that we don't label ourselves with the "bad mom" status because we have a rough day with our kids. It means that we give ourselves grace, and lots of it.

God tells us in Philippians 4:5 that He wants our gentleness to be evident to all. This is in reference to our speech, our actions, and the emotions that we output into the world as we go about each day. So in this confrontational, opinionated world we live in, we have two choices. We can either conform to it and partake in these negative, unhelpful discussions, or we can keep on scrolling. We can choose to rip ourselves and others down or build ourselves and others up. We can choose to be harsh or soft-spoken. *Being gentle is a choice, and one that honors and reflects Christ.*

Mastering Self-Control

"For the Spirit God gave us does not make us timid,
but gives us power, love, and self-discipline."
                                    2 Timothy 1:7

I always think back to Jesus in the desert after He had fasted for forty days and forty nights and was tempted by Satan to turn stones into bread. Of course it sounded appealing even to Jesus because He was human at the time, with human needs and desires. I can only begin to imagine how outrageously hungry and depleted He must have been! But yet regardless, He chose to resist and do the right thing instead. Yes, even though it was incredibly difficult and uncomfortable, Jesus chose to do what was right and resist the enemy.

How can we apply this story of Jesus in the desert to our lives and to being more fruitful? Well, we can start by disciplining ourselves to make the necessary choices to better our health, even when it is not easy. Very few people really *want* to wake up before the sun to work out. Very few people *want* to put in the extra work of planning and prepping their meals in order for them to eat more cleanly. No, no one really *wants* to put in the work, but when we are self-disciplined, we JUST DO IT, and we pray each day that we will have the self-control we need not to quit when the going gets tough.

The Bible reminds us to practice self-control and be conscientious of how we feed our bodies. Proverbs

25:16 says, "Do you like honey? Don't eat too much, or it will make you sick!" God isn't saying that we can't enjoy life, but He is saying that we must practice self-control and not overindulge. Remember the 80/20 principle we talked about? A healthy life is all about moderation and balance. A healthy life is all about making healthy choices to better our body, even when it isn't easy.

So maybe you pass on the soda and order water instead, or you wake up early to squeeze in a work-out instead of sleeping in. Or maybe you decide to stay in and cook a healthy, balanced meal for your family instead of ordering greasy takeout. It doesn't matter how big or how small. Every single choice we make adds up! Choosing to make the healthiest choice for our body may not always be appealing, and it may require effort, but if you persevere, you *will* be blessed with amazing results in the end, and it *will* pay off!

In regards to our spiritual health, God asks us to practice self-control and resist temptation. As human beings, we can be tempted to give in to anger, lust, hatred, jealousy, slander, gossip, laziness, idolatry, and more. We must ask Him daily for strength to resist temptation and reflect His love out into the world. It's easy to give in to the way of the world and be tempted to conform to its ways, but again, God calls us to live *in* this world but not be *of* it.

Growing up, the "WWJD" bracelets were very pop-ular, and I'm pretty sure I had a good dozen of them throughout my childhood. Anyway, those bright rubber bracelets were a reminder for the one wearing one to ask themselves often, "What would Jesus do?" This simple question is the perfect question to ask ourselves as we go about our day while we are making decisions, communicating with others, and caring for our bodies.

"Would Jesus sit here and gossip?"

"Would Jesus spend more money than He had and live outside of His means?"

"Would Jesus hold this grudge?"

"Would Jesus eat junk food on the daily instead of properly nourishing His body with whole foods?"

"Would Jesus envy others for what they had and what He didn't have?"

"Would Jesus yell and flip off the car that cut Him off in traffic?"

"Would Jesus go into this negative rampage on social media?"

...The answer is a resounding "no"!

We, as humans, will sin and give in to temptation from time to time. It is just inevitable. That being said, if we ask God to give us the strength to practice self-control in every area of our lives and keep us from falling into temptation, He will. In fact, God promises this in 1 Corinthians 10:13, where it says, *"No temptation has overtaken you except what is common to mankind. And God is faithful; he will not let you be tempted beyond what you can bear. But when you are tempted, he will also provide a way out so that you can endure it."*

But here's the kicker. God will give us the strength to do what is right, but it is up to *us* to utilize this strength and practice self-control. It is up to us to do the work and put the time in. It is up to us to do what is right and healthy, even when it is difficult. It is a choice. God does not promise us that a righteous life following Him will be an easy one, but He does promise us that it will be a rewarding one. So, pray each morning as you rise for God to give you the strength to practice self-control as you go about your day. Care for yourself and others in a way that will honor God, and never stop asking yourself this one very powerful question: *"What would Jesus do?"*

Embracing the Woman You Were Meant to Be

If you are a mother and you are reading this, then hear me out when I remind you once again how incredibly blessed you are! God chose YOU to grow, nurture, and raise your precious children because He knew they needed *you* specifically and no one else. God foresaw the trials that you would go through, and He knew that you could handle them. He knew that you were equipped to not just be a mother but to be *their* mother. He never doubted your ability for a second. But one thing He didn't do is ask you to put yourself last, stop using your gifts, and lose sight of the amazing and beautiful woman you are.

You are now a mother, but you are still *you*. You are a unique person and an individual that God wants to use in many, many ways. He entrusted us with children to raise, a husband to love, and a home to take care of, and so much more. But the thing is, the enemy is threatened by us. He is scared because he sees us as mothers, raising up this next generation, and he wants nothing more than to hinder us from doing our job. He wants to keep us exhausted and worn thin. He wants to keep us depressed and in a pit. He wants to keep us from teaching our children about the love of Jesus. But we must fight back and keep ourselves strong so that he doesn't win.

Ladies, we cannot afford to burn out! We cannot afford to put ourselves last and lose our steam because God and our families are counting on us! They deserve the best version of us, so we cannot let our physical, mental, or spiritual health go, can we? No! We must care for ourselves daily. We must nurture our mind, body, and soul and ensure that we are strong for the tasks that God has laid down before us to do.

Self-care is complex. It has such a negative stigma around it these days, but let me remind you that it is NOT selfish but incredibly necessary. *Self-care is vital if we want to thrive and not merely survive.* Self-care only is possible, though, if we practice intentional living and make it a point to keep ourselves at the top of our priority ladder, regardless of how hectic life gets. Self-care sometimes can mean saying "no," spending time in prayer, asking others for help, eating more whole foods and less sugar, taking a nap, walking away from a toxic friendship, taking time away to pursue a hobby, and so much more.

Self-care can really mean something different for everyone. *Self-care is whatever leaves you feeling like the best, most refreshed version of you.* Self-care is whatever makes you feel whole and renewed. Self-care is whatever gives you the strength to face each day and the ability to better love others. Self-care is your gift to your children and those you love. Self-care is KEY to living your best life. So whatever you do, never stop loving and caring for yourself, and allow me to remind you one last time that *Mama, You Still Matter!*

With Love,
Laura